AF291919

POLITICS, POLICY and PREDICTIONS

Also by Derek O'Brien

Inside Parliament: Views from the Front Row

POLITICS, POLICY AND PREDICTIONS

Views from the Front Row
of Parliament

DEREK O'BRIEN

HarperCollins *Publishers* India

First published in India by HarperCollins *Publishers* 2026
HarperCollins *Publishers* India, Cyber City,
Building 10-A, Gurugram, Haryana – 122002, India
www.harpercollins.co.in

2 4 6 8 10 9 7 5 3 1

P-ISBN: 978-93-6569-110-8
E-ISBN: 978-93-6569-894-7

Typeset in 11.5/14.9 Arno Pro
by HarperCollins *Publishers* India

Printed and bound at
Manipal Technologies Limited, Manipal

This book is produced from independently certified FSC® paper to
ensure responsible forest management.

HarperCollins *Publishers*, Macken House, 39/40 Mayor Street Upper, Dublin 1,
D01 C9W8, Ireland

*To Father Stan Swamy and all the other brave hearts who
sacrificed their lives fighting the good fight*

The detailed notes pertaining to this book are available on the HarperCollins website. Scan this QR code to access the same.

Contents

CONTENTS

POLITICS

MEDIA

SPEECHES

PROLOGUE

DECODING THE BODY LANGUAGE OF POLITICIANS

Psychologists believe it is an essential assessment tool to understand human behaviour—child therapists suggest that an infant learns to read facial expressions and gestures much before they can even say their first words. Performance artists will tell you it's one of the most natural forms of expression. From boardrooms to brunch tables, from cocktail parties to Parliament, every single space of interaction is brimming with a rich quotient of 'metadata' called body language.

Amongst all such spaces, one of the most promising and intriguing fora for this data is the world of electoral politics. During the run-up to the 2024 US elections, when a Presidential candidate made outlandish remarks about immigrants on a live television debate, his opponent's non-verbal responses flooded everyone's social media timelines. Memes, GIFs and stickers were churned out in real time. In the same campaign, a former Vice President's communications team released a commercial scripted around the love lives of black voters. These aren't just one-off cases from a country across the Pacific Ocean. The scene in India is no different.

Even his harshest critics will grudgingly concede that Narendra Modi assuming responsibility as the country's Prime Minister in 2014 was, what marketeers call, a moment of truth (MoT)—when a user interacts and forms a different opinion about a product. Since Independence, one cannot think of any Chief Ministers of a state who was as brilliantly packaged and then catapulted into the post of PM in this manner. Various iconic chief ministers—Dr B.C. Roy, Biju Patnaik, M. Karunanidhi, Sucheta Kripalani, Vasantrao Naik—were never profiled as potential Prime Ministerial candidates before Lok Sabha elections. But the marketing kit put together for Modi's first run as Prime Minister focused on ancillaries that made for good television and catchy sound bites. Teaseller to champion CM. The sevak who gave up friends, and having a wife and family in favour of selfless service. The success story of the Gujarat model of development amplified on the banks of the holy river in Varanasi. His four-hour sleep schedule. His favourite yoga pose. The bachelor with machismo. Crafted images and ideas that spoke a thousand words each, and then some.

Addressing the audience after the conclusion of the 2024 Ramnath Goenka Excellence in Journalism Awards, the Chief Editor of *The Indian Express*, Raj Kamal Jha, was spot on when he said, 'We have a few maaliks [media moguls] who have gone down on bended knee—so comfortable in that posture that it hurts if they stand up.' Since the time Modi first rose to power, sycophants masquerading as owners of television networks and newspapers have cozied up to the man, the myth, the legend. The iconography and merchandise that has been manufactured makes the classic Nehru coat look like an ill-fitted garment at a fancy dress contest. Welcome to the store now hawking Modi jackets instead, and caps, masks and whatnot. Welcome now to the new Parliament of summer 2024, with the boisterous thumping of desks. The chants louder every day. *Mo-di! Mo-di!* Hero worship projected on the giant screens fitted onto the walls of the Lok Sabha ahead of the General Elections.

On 4 June 2024, were you viewing the live-stream from the Bharatiya Janata Party (BJP) headquarters in New Delhi, when Modi walked on to the stage? (May I suggest you put this book down for a moment and watch the footage first?) The belligerent 'Modi-Modi' chants were not to be heard. As the cameras cut to close-ups of the faithful who had assembled, you could spot the uneasy diffidence on their faces. Stunned faces. The standard 'Bharat Mata Ki Jai' sloganeering was high on volume but low on conviction. The 'Jai Jagannath' chant seemed replaced with the well-rehearsed chorus line of 'Jai Shri Ram'. An awkward long pause preceded Modi's opening remarks. Observers of body language would have noticed an uncharacteristically nervous opening. Over the next thirty minutes, it was like listening to a rockstar with a sore throat and a runny nose; a rockstar having a bad night at Madison Square Garden. The music was playing. But the magic was missing. The crowds knew why.

Notes from that muggy evening from someone who studies body language: no fingers pointing confidently in the air. No trademark squinting eyes to drive home a point. No working the crowd with practised ease. This was negative body language. Even the eponymic 'Modi Ki Guarantee' had a hollow ring to it. The chest thumping simply lacked conviction.

Did the body language improve five days later when the Prime Minister took the oath for his third term? There was a noticeably nervous grip of the lectern. There was a gaze darting rapidly as he checked and rechecked himself in the monitor up ahead. Understandable in 2014, Act One. Inexplicable in 2024, Act Three. The audience seemed subdued too. This was not the 400-seat victory that had been anticipated. Watch the footage carefully. You will notice how the Prime Minister shuffles off stage. Any such quick movement away from the hypocentre of the action indicates that the person is uncomfortable in the circumstances.

Did the body language improve a few days later when the 18th Lok Sabha was convened? As Modi delivered his first speech in Parliament in his third innings as PM, his party colleagues, otherwise cock-a-hoop, were distinctly quieter. The Prime Minister seemed to have picked up the vibe. Instead of the usual swagger, he walked hastily to his seat in the front row. Speech time. No strong launch. No holding for pause. Soon enough, he was drowned out in a different kind of noise. This time, the Opposition was all charged up—cohesive and strong. Over the next hundred and twenty minutes, he was visibly bothered by the vociferous protest from the newly elected Opposition members of parliament (MPs). He flickered his eyes, struggling to be heard. Producers and online editors of Sansad TV are, obviously, well-instructed to cut away from the Treasury bench's weak moments. But even seasoned technicians handling television production may fail to spot politicians exuding dodgy body language at times. The Prime Minister tried his best to deflect from the Opposition's aggression. Pulling off a move practised by experienced orators, he furrowed his eyes to convey how troubling the subject matter of the discourse was. The cameras recorded for posterity, India's 14th Prime Minister doing what body language experts refer to as a 'hard swallow'—an unconscious display of nervousness or anxiety.

~

Months after the election results, front benchers of the BJP still seemed to be on edge. At an election rally in Haryana, the Home Minister shook his fingers nervously. He beckoned the crowd forth but let his desperation show when he said: 'public *ko* camera *tak aa jaane do*' (let members of the public come in front of the camera). As he introduced one of the candidates, another faux pas: '*khade hojao, bhai*, vote *lena hai*' (please stand up, we have to get votes). A stark contrast from previous appearances with hands placed authoritatively on the waist, aggressively taking on the opponents. Amit Shah has been a frequent user of, what analysts call, 'the steeple', where one's fingers are joined together in a V-shape pointing upwards. Public speakers often include 'the steeple' in their gestures to project confidence even when they are feeling under-confident.

Journalists tracking Shah had noticed at the time that the speech he made in an election rally in Haryana was not a one-off blip. At a press conference held to mark the completion of a hundred days of the National Democratic Alliance (NDA) government, a scribe shot straight: 'How is it that the Manipur Chief Minister is continuing [in office] despite so much violence?' Shah's eyes scanned the floor. The discomfort on the interviewee's face was apparent. He pulled his mouth into a tight, over-dramatized smile, feigning composure: 'You can ask questions, but you cannot argue'. This was not the body language you would expect from someone in command of the situation.

Before she became a member of the Rajya Sabha, Nirmala Sitharaman played the role of party spokesperson to perfection. But often enough now, these questions pop up: has her body language and demeanour changed since she became the finance minister? Is she curt in her interactions with the media? Are her interventions in Parliament and her engagement on public platforms unnecessarily combative and downright rude? What happened to the pleasant spokesperson? When asked if the government, now a coalition, would be able to introduce 'bold reforms', the finance minister of the world's fourth largest (apparently) economy could muster the following non-response response: 'We will *certainly* be able to do it'. The use of the word 'certainly' might have convinced the *listener*, but not the *viewer*. This was jittery body language. Fingers interlocked, gripping the microphone almost too hard. Mouth compressed at the corners as this sentence is delivered with disdain: 'There is no need for any apprehension.'

Let me share another example.

While introducing the controversial Waqf Amendment Bill in Parliament, the Minister of Parliamentary Affairs, Kiren Rijiju, did his best to present the Bill as a progressive work of legislation. Rijiju was keen to introduce it by circumventing any discussion and thus avoiding scrutiny. At first, he pretended to respond to the Opposition's dissent, hoping for the chatter to die down quickly. He waved his hands almost as if to placate Opposition MPs, gently chiding them into forgetting how problematic the Bill was. But no one was in the mood to be distracted. The dissent continued. Rijiju's face tensed. The technical description for this would be 'tension in laryngeal thyroid cartilage': a tell-tale sign of anxiety. He adjusted his scarf and went into damage control mode: 'Members of Parliament should not be associated with any religion.' Clutching at proverbial straws.

In all fairness, though, not everyone in the ruling dispensation is showing signs of anxiety. The Union Minister for Agriculture and Farmers Welfare, Shivraj Singh Chouhan, made an impressive debut in Parliament. In his opening speech, the former four-time chief minister countered criticism from the Opposition benches with a self-assured smile, and the mature defence of a seasoned pro. Sitting a few metres away, I observed his stance. He stood with his left shoulder angling outwards. I was intrigued enough to do some digging on this. It turned out, such a posture (angling outward) is an established sign of showing real interest in the conversation one is a part of. Chouhan combined his interest in the debate with postulation. He made focused arguments using what experts refer to as a 'precision grip'. This is when one joins the thumb and the index finger to convey accuracy. Worked well.

Another person from the ruling dispensation who continues to be on the good side of body language experts is the Minister of Road, Transport and Highways, Nitin Gadkari. Gadkari has mastered the art of handling the media with comfort. We often see him stopping by the entrance to Parliament to informally interact with journalists. He does this without any pretensions, a style not shared by most of his colleagues in the Union cabinet. Gadkari seems to welcome pointed questions and smilingly responds even to rumours—always low on arrogance and high on politeness. The questions might be discomforting, but Gadkari rarely gets worn down. Eyes wide open, yet relaxed, gesticulating passionately to explain his point punctuating his comments with his quintessential chuckle—wish his colleagues in the ruling party were also more like him.

As this book goes to press, a thirty-four-year-old is sworn-in as the mayor of New York City in the United States of America. Headlines and tickers run and re-run the many historic firsts he has achieved. Pundits ponder upon the 'spillover effect' that the result has already had and will continue to have on American politics in the time to come. Analysts comb through metrics behind the 'voter funded, door-to-door' campaign. Opinion pieces are being written to decode a campaign that is being perceived as a masterclass in communications. All well deserved. However, at an oddly specific point during the candidate's victory speech, fixated as I was on my iPad screen, I realized why I wanted to write about body language in my new book.

Around the seventeenth minute of his speech, New York City's new Mayor makes direct eye contact with the camera. There is an obvious increase in his decibel level. He takes a second to steady himself. Then there is a slight shift in the way he's standing—almost as if to make *you* more comfortable with what he is about to say. And then, roaringly: 'So, Donald Trump, since I know you're watching, I have four words for you—turn the volume up!' The crowd erupts in applause. The speaker stays steady, composed. The applause continues, now with a ringing effect in the audio transmission. And then, when he knows the intended effect has been achieved, he breaks into a smile—sure-footed as ever, almost proclaiming his own graduation from 'new kid on the block' to statesman. Allow me to stick my neck out and say what no analysis has so far: the confidence and conviction in his ideas, as seen in this moment, is precisely what carried him to victory.

Now, a contrast. New Delhi. Rajya Sabha. March 2025. Topic of discussion? The functioning of the Union government's home ministry. A young MP of the Opposition begins to make his arguments. Almost immediately, a minister rises to interrupt. At first, a deliberate slowing down of speech and volume. Then, jaw clenching, glaring the MP down: *'I will answer everything'*. The MP remains undeterred and continues. Then: a second attempt at bullying the speaker. This time facing the MP, squinting. Wagging his finger in the air angrily, his voice almost quivering: *'I have won seven elections! The question of getting scared does not arise.'* Desperate. Threatened. Union Minister Amit Shah.

His misplaced attempts at intimidation aside, Shah comes across a bit differently outside Parliament. He sits in interviews almost shrunk in his seat. Arms and legs tightly crossed, foot tapping the floor in nervous impatience. The voice is uncharacteristically low, as if to simulate humility. His gaze flutters across the room as he *tries* to field a question, and if you force yourself to watch long enough, you catch him shutting his eyes, struggling to recall the answers rehearsed to perfection in the wings. Demure. Unassured. Timid.

Across political discourse, there is abundant commentary that decodes 'stance' and 'strategy'. An even greater volume of data that 'projects' and 'predicts'. Lost in all of this? The person behind the politics. Reading *them* will always reveal to you what no other resource can. So, the next time you see your favourite—or even not so favourite—politician making a speech in Parliament, don't only listen to what they're saying. Instead, watch what their bodies are saying.

POLICY

1

Safe Drinking Water: A Fundamental Right

Safe drinking water is not only crucial to human health and well-being but access to it is also a fundamental right protected under the ambit of the Right to Life (Article 21) in the Constitution.

India has about 18% of the world's total population, but only 4% of its water resources.[1] This makes us one of the most water-stressed countries in the world. Many Indians face high to extreme water stress caused by lack of availability and/or poor quality of available water, according to the NITI Aayog as well.[2] On top of that, chemical pollution of water remains a health burden, whether natural in origin (arsenic or fluoride) or anthropogenic. It affects livelihood, school attendance, standard of living, people's dignity and the environment.

More than 60% of households do not treat their water before drinking.[3] According to the United Nations Children's Fund (UNICEF), only a fourth of the total population in the country has drinking water in their households.[4] As per a 2017 World Bank report, it is estimated that about one-fifth of all communicable diseases in India are water related.[5] As per the Ministry of Health and Family Welfare, it is estimated that seven out of ten disease outbreaks in India are because of water.[6] About 38% of children under the age of five are stunted, and 50% of malnutrition cases are linked to diarrhoea.[7] Around thirty diseases are a consequence of unsafe water, poor sanitation and hygiene.[8] According to the National Family Health Survey (NFHS-5), diarrhoea was prevalent in 7.3% children under five years of age.[9]

The existing sources of data for tracking water and its safety are the Census, National Family Health Survey and Integrated Management Information System. The first two do not dwell upon the quality and reliability of water, and the third lacks data on sufficiency of water and is not standardized and comprehensive enough for rural areas. Delay in the Census and data gaps such as these provide a big lacuna in managing water resources to the optimum level. There is an urgent need to strengthen and standardize existing reporting, and expand the scope of surveys to cover more indicators of safely managing the drinking water services. This is critical to good policymaking and planning of welfare schemes.

All individuals should be entitled to clean water and sanitation without any discrimination. Marginalized populations, including women, children and refugees, are frequently disregarded by and excluded from access to supply of safe drinking water, based on their societal positioning.

Article 14(2)(h) of the Convention on the Elimination of All Forms of Discrimination against Women (CEDAW) provides: 'States parties shall take all appropriate measures to eliminate discrimination against women in rural areas in order to ensure, on a basis of equality of men and women, that they participate in and benefit from rural development.' But the burden of water collection often falls on women who have to travel long distances and stand in long queues to fetch water. This has direct consequences on their school attendance, ability to work, childcare, etc., and thrusts them to the front of verbal, sexual and physical violence and discrimination by societies.

Caste plays an important role in the denial of access to safe drinking water in public spaces and is a big manifestation of the existence of social discrimination. More than 20% of Dalits lack access to safe drinking water and often face violence for trying to access these resources.[10] Harmful concepts of purity and contamination continue to govern the thinking of individuals in affected areas, even after untouchability has been abolished.

The Union government controls the regulation and development of inter-state rivers, which are a major source of water in India. Making these channels safe for drinking needs to be prioritized. Even the Jal Jeevan Mission that aims to provide tap water in every household misses out on making this water safe for drinking. Such weak systems and lack of funding from the Union government have hindered the reach in India. India's water sector has faced an investment gap of 21 lakh crore rupees between 2015–2030 according to the G20 (Group of 20) Infrastructure Outlook.[11]

Hence, there is a need to make the sector more attractive for investment, along with increasing the budgetary allocation specifically for making drinking water safe, so that states can make a bigger difference. The issue of access to clean drinking water cannot be looked at in isolation. It is dependent on other factors of gender, class, caste and education, among others. Involvement of stakeholders in the making of policies at each level is imperative in minimizing the discrimination in such access.

2

ODISHA TRAIN COLLISION: THE RED FLAGS THE BJP GOVERNMENT IGNORED

Telangana, 2014: 20 dead.[12] *Rae Bareli, 2015: 32 dead.*[13] *Kanpur, 2016: 150 dead.*[14] *Andhra Pradesh, 2017: 40 dead.*[15]

In an answer given to Parliament in July 2022, the Ministry of Railways stated that there were a total of 244 'consequential' train accidents between 2017 and 2022.[16]

May 23 2023: 'The all-around work to transform the railways began only after 2014. Everyone was clueless before this. So how could they even think about high-speed trains?'

—The Prime Minister of India[17]

June 3 2023: Balasore Coromandel train collision in Odisha. 288 families grieve the loss of their loved ones. 1,000 families traumatized.[18]

Balasore was an accident waiting to happen.

Notably, the self-indulgent photo ops for the Vande Bharat inaugurations have not aged well. India's passenger trains are still neglected and are often resigned to function like mobile mortuaries. On the floor of Parliament, members from Opposition parties have often red-flagged these serious issues and offered constructive suggestions. No one has listened, because PR (public relations) has been prioritized over PS (passenger safety).

On the subject of infrastructure at the cost of safety and maintenance, here is what I had said in Parliament in 2022, 'Your outlook is different from the outlook of the Opposition and many other parties. For us, the Railways constitute the infrastructure for the fundamental right of every Indian citizen to move from point A to point B. It is the fundamental right for transport. You may look at it differently. That bullet train is your vanity project.' Red flag.

No one is opposed to the idea of the bullet train. But what is of concern is the Union government's list of priorities. The cost of one bullet train from Mumbai to Ahmedabad is over 1 lakh crore rupees.[19] Compare this to the Rashtriya Rail Sanraksha Kosh, a fund created specifically for critical safety-related works in the Railways. The five-year budget for this fund is 1 lakh crore rupees![20] Red flag.

A few more red flags: when railway sets were imported from Europe, was proper sequencing done? Was safety blindsided by a reckless infrastructure push? Was maintenance jeopardized because it was a service dog, not a show dog? A scathing report by the Comptroller and Auditor General (CAG) opined that non-priority projects got precedence over maintaining safety standards. Over 50% of the compulsory track safety inspections were not done.[21] Three out of four consequential accidents in the last four years were due to derailment.[22] The ministry admitted in Parliament that over 3 lakh positions in the Railways (gazetted and non-gazetted) are still vacant.[23] Red flag.

Another clear problem is the slow roll-out of anti-collision devices. In 2022, the Ministry of Railways told the Rajya Sabha that 'safety is accorded the highest priority. Indian Railways has indigenously developed an automatic train protection system rechristened as "Kavach" (Train Collision Avoidance System), to prevent accidents due to human error resulting in signal passing at danger and over-spending.[24] (The ministry used the term 'rechristened'! Basically admitting that they had pinched an idea from 2009 and were only packaging it differently.) Of the total Indian Railways route of over 1 lakh kilometres across the country, Kavach has been installed on only 1,445 kilometres so far.[25]

Let me give you another example. The Southeastern Railway division, the route where the Balasore tragedy took place, had not spent a single rupee on anti-collision devices in the three years before the tragedy in 2023, even though an amount of 943 crore rupees was sanctioned.[26]

On 15 February 2023, the official X handle of the Ministry of Railways tweeted that 'Indian Railways production units have ramped up LHB (Linke Hofmann Busch) coach production by manufacturing 4,175 LHB coaches in FY 2022–2023, till 31 January, to ensure convenient and faster mobility.'[27] LHB coaches were deemed to be safer with anti-collision technology, disc brakes, and centre buffer coupling system (absorbing high impacts and preventing flipping of coaches post impact). Both the express trains involved in the tragedy were equipped with LHBs.

It must be also noted that the Vision 2020 document has been blatantly ignored by the authorities. In 2009, the then Minister of Railways, Mamata Banerjee, had tabled the Vision 2020 document in Parliament. Let me quote from Section 6.2 of the document, Safety: Zero Tolerance for Accidents: 'In 10 years, Indian Railways would target to banish accidents from its operations. This would be achieved through a combination of technological and Human Resources interventions. Advanced signalling technology (such as automatic verification of train movement and line occupation through track circuiting/axle counters, train protection systems and anti-collision devices) would be used in combination with training of station and running staff to eliminate collisions.'[28] Little has been done to this end in all this time. Some grim questions remain to be answered.

Postscript: Since 1940, senior government inspectors of Indian Railways have been placed under the administrative control of 'some authority of the Government of India other than the Railway Board'. Guess who the Commission of Railway Safety has submitted the report of the Balasore accident to? The Ministry of Civil Aviation.

3

Government's CoWIN Claims Can Work Only at WhatsApp University

In the summer of 2023, Prime Minister Narendra Modi and two of his ministers were in full damage control mode. The personal information of lakhs of Indians registered on the Union Government's CoWIN portal was leaked. Details of Aadhaar cards, passport numbers, Permanent Account Numbers (PANs) and various other documents were all freely accessible through a Telegram bot. Anyone could easily access details through a basic phone number search.[29]

Despite such a large-scale breach of data on a government platform, the Union government did what it does best—deny and then underplay the violation. Even as the data continued to be widely accessible, the government said, 'The CoWIN portal of the Ministry of Health is completely safe with adequate safeguards for data privacy. Furthermore, security measures are in place on the CoWIN portal.' The statement added that the data being circulated was stolen in the past and was not sourced in that week's breach.[30] An excuse that would only hold good in a class taught at WhatsApp University!

This was not the first data breach on CoWIN. Dismissing the previous attempt made in January 2023, National Health Authority CEO R.S. Sharma had said, 'CoWIN has state-of-the-art security infrastructure and has never faced a security breach. The data of our citizens on CoWIN is absolutely safe and secure.'[31] Five months later, ministers dismissed this colossal breach as 'mischievous' reporting.[32] No lessons learned.

One could not help but observe the BJP's nonchalance towards this massive data breach. After all, this breach of data on servers of government institutions was not the first. In December 2022, five servers of the All India Institute of Medical Sciences (AIIMS) were attacked and 1.3 terabytes of data was encrypted.[33] In a hospital where lakhs of citizens come to access affordable healthcare, services were suspended for a week and sensitive data of 40 lakh patients was lost.[34] There are more such cases.

In 2019, the Army faced two cyberattack attempts every month.[35] Cybersecurity group CloudSEK, responsible for providing cyber threat intelligence to the Indian Government's Computer Emergency Response Team (CERT-In), found that India saw the highest number of cyberattacks on government agencies in 2022.[36]

In addition to its own agencies, the government is failing to prevent these attacks on financial and banking institutions as well. According to an answer furnished by the ministry to Parliament in August, there were 248 successful data breaches on banking institutions between 2018 and 2022.[37] Between January and October 2023, 5,70,000 lakh rupees was lost to cyber frauds. Of this, just 0.072% of the money was recovered.[38] In 2024, financial fraud losses between January and June amounted to 11,300 crore rupees.[39] The worst affected demographic, however, are senior citizens. According to National Cyber Security Coordinator Rajesh Pant, of the 3,500 financial frauds reported daily, senior citizens are the most targeted.[40]

Crimes being carried out digitally are also on an alarming rise. The National Crimes Record Bureau (NCRB) says there were 66,000 reported cases of cybercrimes in 2022.[41] Of these, 20% of cases of cyber blackmail, threats, cyber pornography, obscene sexual materials, cyberstalking, morphing and the creation of fake profiles, are against women.[42] Indian Police Service (IPS) Officer and Special Inspector General, Maharashtra Cyber Department, Yashasvi Yadav substantiated this by calling India the sextortion capital of the world with 500 such cases daily. Of these cases, only 0.5% are taken forward as First Information Reports (FIRs).[43]

Not just women, but children in India are also cyberbullied incessantly.

If the Union government is as technology-forward as it makes itself out to be, it should consider moving beyond PR events and hollow buzzwords like e-Kranti.[44]

4

On Women's Quota: A Reality Check

'Woman, I can hardly express
My mixed emotions at my thoughtlessness
After all, I'm forever in your debt …'

—John Lennon

The Union government passed the Women's Reservation Bill in a special session of Parliament in September 2023. The provisions, however, will come into effect after the next Census and delimitation exercise. The earliest that can happen is by 2034. I, however, belong to a political party that has been advocating for the Women's Reservation Bill for years—make that decades.

As per a report by UN Women, 26% of parliamentarians in single or lower houses are women. Only six countries have 50% or more women in Parliament in single or lower houses—Rwanda, Cuba, Nicaragua, Mexico, New Zealand and, surprise, surprise, the United Arab Emirates.[45] At the current rate of progress, gender equality in national legislative bodies will not be achieved before 2063.[46]

In India, while the female voter turnout increased from 46% in 1962 to 66% in 2024,[47] just 14% of the elected MPs in the 18th Lok Sabha were women[48]—no significant change from 2019. Let's look at women's representation beyond Parliament. The Election Commission is a men-only club. One Chief Election Commissioner (CECs), two Election Commissioners (ECs), six Deputy Election Commissioners (DECs), and not a single female member among them.[49]

On 2 March 2023, in the Anoop Baranwal versus Union of India case, the Supreme Court gave directives on the appointment of the CEC and EC, till the Union government passed a law challenging it.[50] On 10 August, the government sneakily introduced the Chief Election Commissioner and other Election Commissioners (Appointment, Conditions of Service and Terms of Office) Bill, 2023, in Rajya Sabha.[51] The government failed to take the opportunity to include reservation for women in the Election Commission.

This lack of representation is visible across other high posts in public life too. There have been only eleven female judges in the Supreme Court since its inception,[52] and no female Chief Justice of India.[53] Even after nearly eight decades of India's independence, there are only two female judges in the Supreme Court at present. Just 110 out of 763 (14%) judges in high courts are women. And only 36% of subordinate judges were female as per a report published in June 2023.[54]

In 2023, all four toppers of the Union Public Services Commission (UPSC) exam were women.[55] The top twenty-five successful candidates consisted of fourteen women and eleven men.[56] However, data shows that women officers accounted for only one out of ten of the total 11,569 IAS (Indian Administrative Services) officers recruited between 1951 and 2020.[57] Though the number of women IAS officers has been increasing over time, the highest has only been one-third, in 2020. In 2022, the number went down again to one out of four.[58]

The numbers are worse in the police force. The pace of growth has been slow, the share of women officers has increased by just six percentage points in the ten years from 2010. As of January 2021, there were only 2.17 lakh women IPS officers,[59] making up merely 10.5% of police officers in the country.[60] No state in the country has more than 25% of women police personnel. In January 2021, in the

Central Reserve Police Forces (CRPF), women make up just 3.4% of all members across nine specialized forces.[61]

The need to increase women's participation is felt not just in public institutions but in private ones as well. A report[62] by Ernst & Young (EY) revealed that the share of women in senior and managerial positions in India is around15%, and only 9% of firms have women as top managers.[63]

A key to increasing participation and representation of women in institutions is to encourage them to join professional and technical courses in larger numbers. The All India Survey on Higher Education (AISHE) report reveals that the enrolment of women was below 30% in engineering courses and less than 40% in management courses.[64] In the World Economic Forum's Global Gender Gap Index 2025, India ranks a dismal 131 out of 146 countries.[65]

5

What Happened to PM's 'People in Chappals in Havai Jahaz' Dream

'I want to see people who wear Hawaii chappal in a *havai jahaz*.'
—Prime Minister Narendra Modi

Clever line.

On 21 October 2016, the Prime Minister said this while inaugurating one of the Union Government's dream projects—affordable regional air connectivity from one part of the country to another. Or the Regional Connectivity Scheme—Ude Desh Ka Aam Nagrik (UDAN) scheme.

Smart acronym.

Unlike the dozens of other forgettable acronyms created since 2014, I like the name UDAN. But let's examine whether it has really taken off or been grounded in the last few years. Are those citizens who can only afford Hawaii chappals, really being transported from Point Mo to Point Di in a *havai jahaz?*

A report by the Airport Council International depicted that India witnessed the highest rise in airfare in the Asia-Pacific region post the pandemic. The airfares went up by nearly 41%.[66]

16

In 2023, when a major private operator filed for bankruptcy, it did not help the sector in any way either.[67] It caused an upward pressure on prices due to increased demand and left the market at the mercy of the remaining operators. It is not a stretch to say that the aviation sector is a budding duopoly benefitting plutocrats, ignoring Hawaii chappals.

The government still needs to adopt the recommendations made recently by the Parliamentary Standing Committee on Transport, Tourism and Culture. Till date, airfares are determined based on the Aircraft Rules of 1937,[68] which implies that airlines can fix the prices based on the tariffs, keeping reasonable profits in mind. However, by not defining 'reasonable', the government has enabled airlines to squeeze travellers when it comes to pricing. The completely hands-off approach to regulate prices in the sector has helped private operators to often overcharge customers. Some airlines have even introduced additional charges, such as fuel charges, to compensate for higher prices of Aviation Turbine Fuel (ATF), which accounts for approximately 40% of operating costs.

Adding to this, many of the Union government's decisions under the UDAN-3 are of serious concern. Of the 774 routes awarded under the scheme, 403 routes (52%) could not initiate operations. Of the 371 routes that did start operations, only 112 (30%) could complete the three-year concession period. Of these 112 routes, only 54 (48%) routes could operate beyond three years. This means, only 7% of the initially awarded projects were operational as of March 2023.[69] Questions must be asked of the methodology to award these projects.

The CAG's report on UDAN was scathing. It noted that even after five years, accounting transaction practices in line with prescribed guidelines had still not been established. No rules had been framed by the Ministry of Civil Aviation for collection of payments under the Regional Air Connectivity Fund (RACF)—a corpus fund created especially for airline operations and revenue under UDAN. There is another shocker. The Regional Air Connectivity Fund Trust's accounts were not submitted to the CAG for auditing.[70] (The officers who came up with the CAG Report might have been rewarded for their sterling work. A punishment posting may be on its way!)

Multiple aviation experts I spoke to observed that while the National Civil Aviation Policy of 2016 was touted as a pro-citizen intervention, it was really a ploy by the Union government to hand over India's national carrier to a chosen bidder. The policy diluted what is commonly referred to as Rule 5/20, which mandates five years of domestic operations before operators arc allowed to fly internationally. UDAN short-circuited this requirement. As a result of this, by utilizing 20% of the airline's total aircraft capacity, any airline can conduct international operations.[71] In one fell swoop, the government removed all checks and balances which were needed for private players to ply with, on more profitable international routes. The Maharaja is dead. Long live the self-proclaimed king.

6

CREAKING INFRASTRUCTURE AND AN ABSENT BJP GOVERNMENT

'As I walked around the site, I thought that these days the biggest temple and mosque and gurdwara is the place where man works for the good of mankind. Which place can be greater than this, this Bhakra–Nangal, where thousands and lakhs of men have worked, have shed their blood and sweat and laid down their lives as well? Where can be a greater and holier place than this, which we can regard as higher?'

—Jawaharlal Nehru
From the speech delivered at the opening of the Nangal Canal
on 8 July 1954

'Bhakra–Nangal is a landmark not merely because the water will flow here and irrigate large portions [of land] or because enough electric power will be generated here to run thousands of factories and cottage industries which will provide work for the people and relieve unemployment. It is a landmark because it has become the nation's will to march forward with strength, determination and courage.'

—Jawaharlal Nehru; at the same location, 1954

'Bhakra–Nangal Project is something tremendous, something stupendous, something which shakes you up when you see it. Bhakra, the new temple of resurgent India, is the symbol of India's progress.'

—Jawaharlal Nehru
Speech at the inauguration of the Bhakra Dam on
22 October 1963

Read these lines. Re-read them. And then snap into the reality of Indian infrastructure. Today. More than sixty years on.

ROADS

In 2023, the Parliamentary Committee on Rural Development called out the PM Gramin Sadak Yojana for inordinate delays and poor-quality construction. While the Union government promised to connect rural settlements to schools, hospitals and agricultural markets through the project, more than 28% of roads still awaited completion.[72]

As of August 2024, Phase 1 of the Bharatmala project had achieved just 50% of its original target. The estimated amount that had already been sanctioned for the project is 58% more than the estimated cost.[73] There is no further update on the costs incurred since this last report.

TUNNELS

Manjeet Lal was trapped in the Uttarkashi tunnel for seventeen days. His elder brother met a tragic fate at a construction site in Maharashtra in 2022. Manjeet's father, who had no mobile phone, or money, spent his time anxiously praying outside a temple near the tunnel. Little did he know that the same company that had faced charges when a launcher collapsed on the Samruddhi Expressway in Mumbai, killing twenty workers, was awarded a project of such importance.[74]

Bridges and Flyovers

While searching for survivors of the Morbi bridge collapse, rescuers found the hand of a child, frozen, tightly clutching a toy, visible through the murky waters. The toy belonged to two-year-old Duruk, who was, perhaps, on one of his first family holidays.

The bridge on the Machchhu river collapsed in October 2022, killing 135 people, including fifty children. The cause of the accident, which was the biggest civic disaster in Gujarat's history, was later found to be gross negligence on the part of the authorities.[75] Just eight months later, a portion of the newly constructed bridge collapsed on the Mindhola river. Preliminary investigation reported serious defects in the quality of materials used by the company that has built several bridges in south Gujarat.[76] In October 2023, another bridge in Palanpur collapsed due to 'workmanship errors', killing two people.[77] Among the victims was an autorickshaw driver, caught under the debris while trying to escape.

After the tunnel collapse in Madhya Pradesh's Sleemanabad in February 2022, Goralal, a construction worker, left a poignant message with his co-worker: 'Tell my mother that I will be born to her in my next life.'

In August 2022, the 304 crore–rupee Karam Dam suffered seepage and erosion, leading to the evacuation of eighteen downstream villages.[78] Notably, the construction company involved is alleged to have ties to the BJP. A scam related to the e-tendering of the dam has been under investigation for the past four years.[79] Interestingly, just three months later, the same blacklisted companies were given contracts for repair and maintenance.[80]

Railways

The Indian Railways constitute the infrastructure to aid the fundamental right of every Indian citizen to travel from point A to point B. Now who wouldn't want a bullet train? But let's put the priorities into perspective. Constructing each route kilometre of the vanity project, that is the bullet train, costs around 200 crore rupees. A dedicated freight corridor, which moves basic commodities for farmers and consumers, has a construction cost of 23 crore rupees per kilometre.

There are so many other examples of poor infrastructure affecting the lives of millions in India. In the first seven months of 2024 alone, there were at least three major railway accidents, claiming the lives of over twelve people. Between 2017 and 2022, a total of 244 train accidents occurred.[81] A report by the CAG points out that over 50% of the compulsory track safety inspections were not completed.[82]

Priorities.

7

HERE'S TO TRIBALS AND THEIR ENDLESS FIGHT FOR JAL, JUNGLE, ZAMEEN

In June 2024, a young MP from the Bharat Adivasi Party, representing Banswara, led a unique march.[83] His supporters carried blood samples to protest a BJP minister's remark that he should perform a DNA test to prove he was Hindu. The young MP stood firm—they were Adivasis who didn't need a DNA test to verify their identity.

Let us explore an often-ignored issue: tribal rights in the last decade of the ruling dispensation.

To begin with, here's how the Ministry of Tribal Affairs fared in the Union Budget 2025:

- The word 'Scheduled Tribe' was not mentioned even once in the speech.
- Allocations for the National Commission for Scheduled Tribes—a constitutional body—reduced from 20.29 crore rupees to 19.68 crore rupees.[84]
- Development of Particularly Vulnerable Tribal Groups (PVTGs) received only 20 crore rupees in 2024, but in 2025, this number went down to zero!

Displacement and Dispossession

According to the Xaxa Committee on Tribal Communities, over 40% of those displaced by development projects are tribals.[85] The Forest (Conservation) Amendment Act, 2023, was rushed through the Lok Sabha in just thirty-eight minutes, with only four MPs participating.[86]

This Act weakened clearance requirements and gave blanket exemptions, impacting forests, wildlife and indigenous communities. Procedurally, the Bill should have been sent to the Ministry of Environment, Forest and Climate Change for scrutiny. Instead, it was sent to a Joint Parliamentary Committee, which was packed with BJP MPs. The committee approved all amendments, despite six MPs submitting dissent notes.[87]

Between June 2022 and July 2024, over 1,000 projects received forest clearances, while only six projects were denied clearance between 2018 and 2022.[88] Interestingly, at least four companies that topped the list of electoral bond donors are notorious for violating forest and tribal rights.[89]

Questions in Parliament have revealed that the Great Nicobar Project worth 72,000 crore rupees will lead to a felling of 10 lakh trees and alter the face of the Ecologically Sensitive Area.[90]

Consider this:

- The Tribal Council of Nicobar Island withdrew its no-objection certificate for the project.[91]
- The government has not consulted the original inhabitants—the Shompens (a PVTG tribe) and the Nicobarese.[92]
- The Anthropological Survey of India was not consulted either.

Misgovernance

Speaking in Lok Sabha, the finance minister claimed that the BJP government secured the rights of people from the Scheduled Tribes

(STs) in India. But the situation on the ground tells a different story. As of October 2025, the Eklavya Model Residential Schools have more than 7,000 vacancies across the country.[93] Announced in the 2022-23 budget, the Venture Capital Fund for Scheduled Tribes (VCF-ST) was not operational until early 2025.[94] It was eventually initiated, but as of March 2025, only two applications had been accepted.

Socioeconomic indicators for the ST population in India are also worrying. As per the National Family Health Survey 2019–21 (NFHS-5), six out of ten ST women and seven out of ten ST children are anaemic. Four out of ten children over six years of age have had no schooling. Five out of ten of the ST population belong to the lowest wealth quintile.[95] In 2023, crimes against STs increased by nearly 30%, with Manipur and Madhya Pradesh recording the highest number of assault cases on ST women and children.[96]

Homogenization

In 2022, the National Commission for Scheduled Tribes (NCST) published a book titled *Contributions of Tribal Leaders in the Freedom Struggle*. The book, which faced sharp criticism for downplaying Adivasi resistance to caste structures, is a replica of an e-book by the Akhil Bharatiya Vanvasi Kalyan Ashram (ABVKA, a Rashtriya Swayamsevak Sangh [RSS] affiliate focused on organizing religious events in tribal areas). At the time, the NCST was led by a former member of the ABVKA. In fact, both BJP and RSS commonly refer to the ST population as 'Vanvasi' (forest dweller) rather than 'Adivasi' (original inhabitants), which reflects their long-standing stance. The ABVKA runs 21,000 projects in more than 16,000 tribal areas, most of which are religious in nature.[97]

The 2024 Lok Sabha elections presented these numbers:

In forty-seven ST reserved constituencies, the BJP's seat count fell from thirty-two in 2019 to twenty-four in 2024, while the Opposition's rose from six in 2019 to nineteen in 2024.

Adivasi communities in Hasdeo, Singrauli, Talabira, Gare Pelma, Chhindwara and elsewhere are resisting the takeover of their jal, jangal and zameen—water, forest and land.

We stand by them as they fight the good fight.

8

Basket of Empty Promises

The President's Address in the 2024 Interim Budget Session was the first of its kind to be delivered in the Lok Sabha, and not the Central Hall of Parliament. That is like playing a key tennis match at Wimbledon on (a new) Court One and not the iconic Centre Court.

I have swotted up the President's Address speeches delivered in the last ten years. Here is a list of eight terms repeatedly used by this government in the last decade that hardly got a single mention in the speech that they wrote in 2024.

Doubling farmers' income: 'My government is striving day and night to attain the goal of *doubling farmers' income.*' President's Address, 2019

No actual assessment of farmers' incomes has been carried out by the Union government since 2013. Incomes needed to grow by 10% year-on-year from 2015 in order to double by 2022. In reality, the growth in farmers' incomes has been around 3.5%.[98] Pipe dreams. Thirty people involved in the farming sector committed suicide every day in 2022.[99]

Bullet train project: 'My government is committed to the construction of world-class Railways. Work on the Mumbai–

Ahmedabad high-speed bullet train has commenced.' President's Address, 2018

With much ballyhoo, the Mumbai–Ahmedabad bullet train project's bhoomi pujan ceremony was held in 2017. Despite initially setting a completion target for the year 2022, subsequent reports indicated a shift in deadlines, particularly for the Vapi–Sabarmati section. Now it is slated for completion by 2027, a ten-year delay. Concurrently, the project cost has surged, from the initial estimate of 1.08 lakh crore rupees to 2 lakh crore rupees.[100]

Swachh Bharat Mission: 'It is our collective responsibility to pay a befitting tribute to pujya Bapu by making the country swachh by 2019, when we celebrate the 150th birth anniversary of the Father of the Nation, Mahatma Gandhi.' President's Address, 2018

After all the hype and hoopla, this was reduced to just one sentence in the 2024 address. In an answer to a question in Rajya Sabha in 2023, the Ministry of Social Justice and Empowerment stated that 308 persons have died while undertaking hazardous cleaning of sewers and septic tanks in the last five years. This, despite the fact that manual scavenging has been banned in the country since 2013.

Demonetization: 'To combat the evils of black money, corruption, counterfeit currency and terror financing, my government took the decision on 8 November, 2016, to *demonetize* old five hundred- and one-thousand-rupee currency notes.' President's Address, 2017

Demonetization was an act of economic terrorism that failed to achieve its stated objectives. Black money, counterfeiting, or terrorism, have certainly not been reduced, leave alone eliminated. Ninety-nine per cent of demonetized currency was returned.

Smart Cities Mission: 'My government has initiated the Smart Cities programme, envisaging city development in a challenge mode.' President's Address, 2016

Launched in 2015 but consigned to oblivion in the President's Address in 2024. Full of buzzwords like innovation, integration, convergence, but no concrete definition of what actually constitutes a smart city. Between 2015 and 2021, of the thirty-three cities selected in the first round (including fast-track), the Union government released no funds to two cities for four years, thirteen cities for three years, twelve cities for two years, and five cities for one year.[101]

Namami Gange: 'An Integrated Ganga Conservation Mission has been set up with a budgetary allocation of more than 2000 crore.' President's Address, 2015

Launched in 2014, this scheme's target was to clean the Ganga by 2019.

Fact 1: Pollution levels in the river are higher than the levels recorded in 2014.

Fact 2: The highest concentration of microplastic pollutants was found in the Prime Minister's own constituency, Varanasi.

Fact 3: The National Ganga Council formed in 2016, and headed by the PM, held its first meeting only after three years in 2019.

Jobs/unemployment: 'While focusing our attention on manufacturing to create more jobs, my government will continue to work on our formidable strength in the service sector.' President's Address, 2015

In 2024, not a single word about unemployment. The unemployment rate rose to an eight-month high of 9.2% in June 2024.[102] Four out of ten graduates under twenty-five years are unemployed in India.[103] While India will need to create 7 crore jobs over the next ten years, it is projected to create only 2.4 crore jobs.[104]

Sagarmala Project: 'Government has also formulated Sagarmala Project to promote port-led development of the coastal regions and communities.' President's Address, 2015

In 2023, the Parliamentary Standing Committee on Transport, Tourism and Culture had cast a scathing critique on the lacklustre progress of funds utilization within the Sagarmala project. The report noted that the 'actual expenditure is only half of the BE allocation.'[105] As a glaring indictment, during the Demands for Grants 2022-23, the committee underscored that out of the forty-four projects in development, thirty-one projects had not received any funds.[106]

Almost all speeches from Prime Minister Modi's government are jholas of empty promises.

9

Big Poll Promises—But Where Are the Jobs?

In the lead up to the Maharashtra and Jharkhand elections in 2024, campaigns of political parties were focused, from 'Mati, Beti, Roti' and 'Ladki Bahin Yojana', to 'Maiya Samman Yojana' and a youth unemployment benefit scheme. The 8.5 crore voters in the youth and women demographic were believed to be the inflexion point.

But for all the pre-poll promises to youth and women, these statistics told a different story.

- About 75 lakh youth enter the labour force every year in India.[107]
- Youth unemployment rate has been at a high 10% for two years now, in 2023 and 2024.[108]
- One in three youth—neither in education, employment, nor training. Women account for a staggering 95% of this group.[109]
- The urban female unemployment rate for 2023 averaged at nearly 9%. For young urban females, it was 20%.[110]
- In 2022, the unemployment rate was six times higher for individuals with secondary or higher education, and nine

times higher for graduates, than those who could not read or write.[111]

- In 2023-24, the unemployment rate for graduates was at 13%, and postgraduates at 12%.[112]
- Unemployment rate among educated females is among the worst in the country, with 20% of graduates and 22.5% of post-graduates unemployed.[113]
- The Economic Survey reveals that half of all individuals are not ready to be employed upon graduating from college.[114]
- Only four out of ten youth in the workforce possess formal skills.[115]
- The female labour force participation rate is at 32%, compared to 58% for men. In urban areas, it is 28% for women compared to 60% for men.[116]
- The Union government introduced a new internship scheme in October 2024 to reduce the unemployment rate in the country. A top company needs to train 4,000 people a year to achieve the target set by the Union government. Back-of-the-envelope calculations suggest that a private firm will need to spend 20 crore rupees every year to train youngsters. How many companies will?

Even after training, there is no guarantee that the trainees will be retained or find a job in the formal workforce. This is especially worrying since this scheme comes at a time when there have been job cuts by major companies across the globe.

THREE CONSTRUCTIVE SUGGESTIONS

Experts have suggested that a better way to roll out the scheme would have been by engaging Micro, Small and Medium Enterprises (MSMEs) instead of big firms. Interns often gain more practical experience in smaller firms, and these businesses, in turn, benefit from an extra set of hands. Additionally, the likelihood of retaining interns and converting them into medium- to long-term employees would be significantly higher, creating a more sustainable model for both interns and MSMEs. This would also encourage and ease the transition of an own-account establishment (establishment operated without any hired employees) to a hired worker establishment (establishment operated with at least one hired employee), which would benefit the economy more.

To tackle urban unemployment, the Union government should accept what many states have already, and the Parliamentary Standing Committee on Labour had suggested in its 25th report: create an employment guarantee programme for urban areas with special emphasis on women. States like Kerala, Tamil Nadu, Jharkhand, Telangana and West Bengal already run similar schemes.

An urban unemployment guarantee programme will be a step in line with Right to Livelihood, which has been read into Right to Life through judicial interpretation. Moreover, it will be a step towards turning the Right to Work (Article 41), currently a directive principle, into a fundamental right.

Joyce Banda, former President of one of the world's poorest countries, Malawi, put it well, 'The seeds of success in every nation on earth are best planted in women and children.'

10

India Is Failing Its Young

The Union government had sanctioned an Eklavya school near eleven-year-old Sulekha's home. Five years have passed, Sulekha has turned sixteen. The school in her neighbourhood—still not functional. This is true for two out of five schools sanctioned under the Eklavya Model Residential School scheme.[117] Sulekha is forced to enrol in the Kasturba Gandhi Balika Vidyalaya (KGBV) located in an 'educationally backward area'. Her favourite class isn't held because the teacher's position has not yet been filled by the administration that reports to the Union government. As of July 2024, there were over 4,000 vacancies in KGBVs for teachers.[118] The highest vacancies are in Uttar Pradesh. Even for subjects with assigned teachers, classes do not take place daily—teachers are frequently absent. It is common practice that even for a five-day week, teachers take an extra day off.

A Grim Childhood

Even as Sulekha studies at the tenth standard level, she struggles to read texts that a student in the second standard should be able to. She is unable to solve mathematics problems from the third grade level. One out of four rural youth, between the ages of fourteen to eighteen, fourteen to eighteen, demonstrate a similar gap in learning.[119] Research suggests that half the students in this age group are unable to solve arithmetic that is taught in the fifth standard.

More recently, to support her family, Sulekha has been forced to drop out of school. One in every five students is compelled to do so.[120] As an alternative to school education, she enrols herself in the Pradhan Mantri Kaushal Vikas Yojana (PMKVY)—a 'flagship' scheme by the Union government, launched to upskill youth to improve the employment opportunities available to them. Sulekha completes all the requirements of the programme. She is even awarded with a certificate. But nothing changes. Like half of the certificate holders, she finds no job.

Coping with all this pressure at a young age can be traumatic. On paper, teenagers with mental health issues can seek help through Manodarpan, a mental health support helpline launched by the Union government during the pandemic. A good idea, but poorly implemented. Calls to the helpline (844 844 0632) almost always go unanswered. There are just 366 counsellors listed in Manodarpan's directory across the country.[121] The District Mental Health Programme is not better either. Just 1,178 psychiatrists and 513 trained psychologists in total.[122]

Thousands of Sulekhas

Sulekha's story is not a one-off. It is the story of hundreds of thousands of youngsters in India. Thirty-five students commit suicide every day (the actual numbers could be even higher).[123]

Many such students depend on schemes like Samagra Shiksha, which provides for teacher salaries, fees for those enrolled under Right to Education, uniforms and school infrastructure. However, the funds under the scheme for states ruled by non-BJP parties like Tamil Nadu, Kerala, Punjab, West Bengal and, until recently, Delhi have either been stalled or denied.[124] Why? Is it because they objected to a certain suffix in the name of the scheme? The National Education Policy (NEP) 2020 advocates for an allocation of 6% of the Gross Domestic Product (GDP) to education.[125] Good intentions, but the reality is wholly different. In 2023-24, the Union allocated 0.44% of GDP to education. This was reduced to 0.37% in the 2025 Union Budget.[126] Sorry, Sulekha, we failed you.

11

RAIL FAIL—THAT'S THE HEADLINE

Three reactions after the stampede and deaths at the Kumbh Mela on 29 January 2025.

I. Multiple news platforms: A *stampede-like* situation occurred at Kumbh …

II. Uttar Pradesh Chief Minister: 'Between 1 a.m. to 2 a.m., at the akhara route where arrangements were made for the Amrit Snan of the akharas, some devotees crossed over the barricades and were critically injured. They were immediately rushed to hospital where treatment was promptly ensured.'[127]

III. A BJP MP and former Union Minister in Parliament: 'There was a tragedy at the Maha Kumbh. An investigation is underway. We do smell a conspiracy there. When the entire investigation is complete, those behind the incident will have to hang their heads in shame.'[128]

Three reactions after the stampede and deaths at the New Delhi Railway Station on 15 February 2025.

I. Government's *favourite* news agency, quoting Chief Public Relations Officer of Northern Railways: 'There is no stampede (at New Delhi Railway Station). It is only a rumour. Northern Railways was running two planned special trains (for Prayagraj).'[129]

II. A BJP spokesperson's post on X: 'New Delhi railway station as of now' (along with a ten-second video clip showing people walking normally on the platform).[130]

III. Minister for Railways, Information and Broadcasting, Electronics and Information Technology's post on X: 'Situation under control at New Delhi railway station (NDLS). Delhi Police and RPF reached. Injured taken to hospital. Special trains being run to evacuate sudden rush.' And '4 special trains to evacuate this unprecedented sudden rush at NDLS. The rush has now reduced.'[131]

The Union government's standard operating procedure is to first underplay the tragedy. Next, subtly spread misinformation through friendly sections of the media. Then, try to deflect the blame. This pattern is visible even for rail accidents. Recall the Balasore tragedy in 2023, one of India's deadliest train accidents, which led to 296 deaths. While on the subject of railways, here are eight points to consider:

1. Nine out of ten non-suburban rail passengers travel in either second class or sleeper class. Only *one* out of ten non-suburban passengers travels in upper classes, including all air-conditioned classes.[132]

2. Over the past decade, air-conditioned passenger capacity has grown by 190%, while second-class capacity has increased by only 15%.[133]

3. Overcrowding in both trains and railway stations is a pitiful sight. Visuals shared on social media invariably show passengers sitting on the floor, squatting outside toilets, or even hanging precariously from doors and windows.

4. The Union government's pet vanity project is the bullet train. Consider this: each kilometre of the bullet train costs approximately 200 crore rupees to construct. Compare that with a Dedicated Freight Corridor (DFC). A DFC transports commodities like vegetables and rice. Cost of construction: 25 crore rupees per kilometre.[134] What should be the priority?

5. No one is making this up! The Union government actually installed selfie booths at railway stations with Prime Minister Modi's life-size models, at a cost of 6 lakh rupees each.[135]

6. In the last ten years there have been 678 consequential train accidents, resulting in 748 deaths.[136] Out of the 217 consequential accidents between 2017–21, 75% accidents were due to derailments.[137]

7. The Kavach safety system has been deployed on just 1,500 route kilometre, accounting for only 2% of Indian Railways's total 68,000 route kilometre.[138]

8. 92,000 vacancies under the 'safety' category were notified in 2024.[139]

9. After 2017, the BJP government stopped the practice of a separate Railway Budget and subsumed it into the Union Budget.

10. The capital expenditure outlay for Railways in Budget 2025 has been pegged at 2.6 lakh crore rupees, the same as the Union Budget estimates of the earlier year. Funds should have been increased to bolster the safety and security of passengers.[140]

The Indian Railways must strike a balance between commercial viability and social responsibility. As I had said in Parliament: 'Railways constitute the infrastructure for the fundamental right of every Indian citizen to move safely from point A to point B.'

Securing the lives of 650 crore passengers is a full-time job. A part-timer will never be able to keep track.

12

With Child Labour, Law Is Not the Problem—Enforcement Is

Long before I started asking quiz questions or delivering speeches in Parliament, I spent eight years in advertising, in an agency that we often fondly called Ogilvy University. The most memorable four days of those eight years were when, as a junior copywriter, I hung around with the 'father of advertising', David Ogilvy, when he visited India. Precious days. Of all of Mr Ogilvy's (he insisted we all call him David) maxims, my favourite was: 'Big ideas are usually simple ideas.'

In the hurdy-gurdy ride of politics, marketing and communication still remain favourite subjects. On May Day this year, there was a brilliant advertisement that appeared in print. The communication was created by Ogilvy India. The intriguing headline screamed, 'This Labour Day, 7.8 million workers should be laid off.' And then the magical twist in the subhead: 'In a country with 35.6 million unemployed adults, there are 7.8 million children working. Let the adults do the work and let the children go to school.' A Big Idea communicated in a simple, powerful way.

Today, the reality of child labour is grim.

An analysis of the Union government's Periodic Labour Force Survey 2018-19 by the United Nations Children's Fund (UNICEF) revealed that the number of children engaged in child labour in India ranged from 18 lakh (using the national definition), to 33 lakh (using the international definition).[141] Almost half of all working children work within their own family. The agricultural sector engages the most children, followed by the industrial sector, including manufacturing and construction.

Worst forms of labour: The most harmful forms of child labour involve work in dangerous industries or occupations. Children from disadvantaged religious or caste backgrounds, as well as those from impoverished households, are more likely to be involved in hazardous work. Abuse and mistreatment by employers, especially in factories, is widely reported. This includes physical and verbal abuse, low wages and a lack of access to health services, even when children suffer accidents or injuries. Lack of proper hygiene, sanitation and clean water leads to children becoming easily susceptible to infectious diseases. Working with toxic materials causes long-lasting, sometimes irreversible, illnesses. Sectors that require urgent attention to address the worst forms of child labour include the production of matches and fireworks, glass and leather products, as well as work in brick kilns, coal mines and construction, among others.

Child labour and poverty: As per the International Labour Organization (ILO), 'Child labour is both a cause and consequence of poverty.' Household poverty pushes children into the workforce to earn money. Some take up work to help support the family income, while many are forced to do so just for survival.

Government apathy: Two years ago, I had asked a pointed two-part question to the Minister of Women and Child Development in Parliament: (a) What is the number of working children between the ages of five and fourteen; and (b) What is the number of rural and urban working children, gender-wise? The minister replied to the first part by stating that there were 613 cases registered under the Child and Adolescent Labour (Prohibition and Regulation) Act, 1986, in 2021. The second part of the question went unanswered.[142] The last Census was carried out more than fifteen years ago in 2011. With the 2021 Census seemingly still in cold storage, it is impossible to know exactly how many child labourers there are in the country. Without understanding the magnitude of the problem, it is difficult to find a meaningful solution.

Need for stricter enforcement: Article 24 of the Constitution of India prohibits the employment of any child below the age of fourteen to work in any factory, mine or any other hazardous employment. The Child Labour (Prohibition and Regulation) Amendment Act, 2016, defined working conditions more clearly. The law is not the problem— enforcement is. Last year, fifty-eight children, including twenty girls, were rescued from a distillery in Madhya Pradesh. They were made to work eleven-hour shifts every day, hardly paid wages, and the palms of their hands were burnt from working with chemicals.[143]

I started on a personal note. Let me end on one. In 2012, as part of the Indian delegation to the 67th session of the United Nations General Assembly in New York, I made a statement on 'Promotion and Protection of the Rights of Children'. Here is what was said: 'The eradication of child labour is a priority for the Government of India. We are strictly enforcing the ban on the employment of children under the age of fourteen years. At the same time, in recognition of the fact that this problem cannot be separated from its socioeconomic circumstances, we are also implementing measures to improve the access to education, health and nutrition for children.'[144]

Thirteen years on, there is still much work to be done.

13

Government Is Not Serious About Human–Animal Conflict

In 2025, Prime Minister Narendra Modi inaugurated Vantara, a wildlife rescue, rehabilitation and conservation centre—also a private zoo. (To offer some perspective, the Delhi Zoo is spread over 200 acres.[145] Vantara is 3,000 acres.[146]) On cue, Virat Kohli, Sachin Tendulkar, Shah Rukh Khan and other high-achiever celebrity friends of Anant Ambani tweeted pictures and praise.

The facility claims to host the world's largest cheetah conservation project. Outside its perfectly manicured precincts, however, the reality is jarring. In the government's nearly 100 crore rupees cheetah relocation exercise[147] in 2022, eight cheetahs and three cubs died.[148] This, according to the government's own admission in Parliament. The exercise was undertaken despite the government's awareness of studies that indicate relocation efforts such as these only have a 50% rate of success. This again, according to its own admission in Parliament.

The challenges surrounding cheetah conservation are just one aspect of a broader attitude of complete abdication of a commitment to protecting wildlife. As per estimates of the Ministry of Environment, Forest and Climate Change, there are currently seventy-three 'critically endangered' species of animals in the country,[149] a sharp rise from forty-seven in 2011.[150]

The critically endangered Great Indian Bustard (GIB) has only about 100 animals left in the wild, according to 2022 government data.[151] In 2021, the Supreme Court ordered the government to take concrete measures to save and conserve the GIB. In its reply, the government stated that the court's orders were 'practically impossible to implement'.[152]

The government's priorities are also reflected in budgetary allocations. Project Tiger and Elephant, which were given separate funding earlier, have now been clubbed together. Funding for these projects declined by 23% between 2019 and 2023, with six states receiving no funds in FY 2022.[153] Another centrally sponsored scheme, Development of Wildlife Habitats, saw a 20% reduction in funding during the same period.[154]

Human–animal conflict is another problem that has not received its due attention. Between 2019 and 2023, elephant attacks caused nearly 2,800 human deaths.[155] In Kerala alone, between 2021 and 2024, conflicts with wildlife claimed 316 lives and injured 3,700 people.[156] During the same period, human–tiger conflicts resulted in nearly 300 deaths, while seventy-five tigers died due to poaching, seizures and other unnatural causes.[157]

Despite the rising toll of human–animal conflict, the government's wildlife management approach has often been reactive and extreme, evident in the continued shoot-at-sight orders issued across states. In 2016, the Union government assured Parliament that no such orders were being issued, only permissions to 'drive the animals away with a stick' in certain cases.[158] However, states have continued with the practice. In 2024, authorities in Uttar Pradesh and Rajasthan ordered the killing of some wolves[159] and leopards[160] in response to attacks on villagers. Likewise, Karnataka[161] took a similar action against a tiger in 2021 due to repeated attacks, while Maharashtra in 2018 decided to kill a tigress based on a court directive.[162]

The government passed the Forest (Conservation) Amendment Bill in 2023. The Bill allowed for sweeping exemptions from forest conservation rules for land located within hundred kilometres of international borders, the Line of Control, or the Line of Actual Control. Despite such critical amendments, it was rushed through the Lok Sabha with only four speakers debating for a little over thirty minutes. The allotted time for discussion: three hours.

The Prime Minister's home state has seen the deaths of 286 lions (fifty-eight unnatural deaths) and 456 leopards (153 unnatural deaths) between 2023 and 2024, as admitted by the Gujarat government.[163] In 2023-24 alone, an average of forty-five animals died in the state's zoos, according to data from the annual reports published by the Central Zoo Authority (CZA).[164] The reports further highlight the poor state of Gujarat's animal care through its rankings. Ahmedabad Zoo received the lowest score among large zoos, and only two out of six zoos in Gujarat were rated 'good' or 'better'. One scored so low that the report specified that it 'requires substantial improvement'.[165]

The one good aspect about philanthropists working on animal welfare is that it will encourage many more to step up. Animals are not a vote bank, which makes them a non-priority for governments. But when high net worth individuals step in with funds, it will help governments scale up the very important work of conservation of wildlife. The other benefit of philanthropists stepping in is the boost it gives to veterinary research. Private funds coming in for animal welfare will encourage greater research in veterinary sciences and encourage more students to take up veterinary medicine as a career.

It is clear that we need a public–private partnership to strengthen conservation, but then it should truly be that—a *partnership*. Private philanthropy shall conserve, support research and create examples with the ultimate goal of strengthening state institutions and not just creating a private enterprise with little or no public accountability.

Seventy years ago, George Orwell wrote in his book *Animal Farm*: 'All animals are equal but some animals are more equal than others.'

FEDERALISM

1

WHO WILL GOVERN THE GOVERNORS?

Tamil Nadu. Kerala. Delhi. Telangana. Punjab. West Bengal. Maharashtra (till 2022). These states have seen a lot of news smouldering in their Raj Bhavans and governors overstepping their mandates. From trying to topple a democratically elected state government in Maharashtra to interfering in the functioning of elected governments; from withholding assent for Bills passed by the House and going off-script in the Tamil Nadu assembly to holding political and provocative press conferences in Kerala, the list of improprieties is long.

WHAT IS THE ROLE OF THE GOVERNOR IN OUR CONSTITUTION?

Articles 153 to 163 of the Constitution provide for a governor appointed for each state by the President, who exercises the executive power of the state. Under Article 164, the Chief Minister is appointed by the governor, and other ministers are appointed by the governor on the advice of the chief minister. The governor thus has a dual role—as the representative of the Union government in the state, and as the constitutional head of the state acting on the advice of the Chief Minister.

This makes it sound like this constitutional functionary has wide, sweeping powers. But the interpretation is not so. A seven-judge bench of the Supreme Court in the Shamsher Singh versus State of Punjab case—as far back as 1974—clarified that governors are to exercise almost all their powers on the chief minister's advice, and are in no circumstances to conduct a parallel government.

Ordinarily, the few instances when a titular head can exercise his discretion are in grave situations, like a hung election result or if the council of ministers loses the confidence of the House. However, while the President has this limited set of discretionary powers, the governor has powers such as reserving Bills for the President's consideration, recommending President's Rule in a state, and calling on the chief minister to seek information on the functioning of the state. In the recent past, some governors seem to have taken this too seriously, even calling for information directly from the civil service officers of the government.

A major concern arises from the fact that the governor is appointed by the President. There are no grounds mentioned in the Constitution for the removal of a governor, and they hold their positions at the discretion of the President. This, of course, means that the Union government has the power to decide who will be the highest constitutional authority in each of the states. And we have seen what happens if it is a state with a non-BJP chief minister.

We live in an era where a politician campaigning for the BJP in Kerala is appointed governor of Mizoram and then called back to Kerala to fight another election. What happened to independent, dignified, constitutional gubernatorial functioning?

The Ranjit Singh Sarkaria Commission of 1983 is considered the gold standard on Union–state relations. It recommended that governors be eminent persons from outside the state, who were not in active politics immediately before their appointment. Additionally, that they be appointed in consultation with the chief minister, Vice President and Lok Sabha Speaker, and their term of office be virtually guaranteed to protect their independence. Finally, it also suggested that governors be ineligible for positions post retirement. Sadly, most of these recommendations have been junked.

Even the Constituent Assembly debates show that many leaders considered governors to be vestiges of India's colonial past. Rohini Kumar Chaudhuri stated that it seemed as if the governor in the Constitution was the same governor who represented the British ruler. H.V. Kamath was concerned that even if the governor is given no express functions to perform, he will be able to prevent the elected government from functioning by using his duties of granting approval. Many members pointed out that the words of the Articles related to governors were almost a reproduction of sections in the Government of India Act of 1935.

To ensure the independent functioning of governors, there is a need to revise Article 157 of the Constitution, and pinpoint more specific criteria and qualifications for the appointment of governors. Since the Article only requires them to be Indian citizens over thirty-five years of age, the field is left too wide for political appointees.

Let's take the advice of B.R. Ambedkar: 'The Constitution is but a skeleton, the flesh has to be put by all of us every day.'

2

India's 'Federalism Dividend' Can Soar Through Innovation

Creativity and innovation influence every aspect of human development. Innovation is not just a buzzword for Big Tech or Fortune 500 companies. My favourite story of innovation is about the little-known engineer Nils Bohlin. While working at Volvo, he invented the V-type three-point safety belt for cars in 1959. Even though Volvo spent millions of dollars in research and development and marketing, they decided not to enforce their patent, and made the design available to all car manufacturers. They prioritized public safety over profits.

At its core, innovation is what makes lives simpler for people from every section of society. It leads to income generation, job creation, inclusive social development and an all-round better quality of life.

Here are some truly inspirational schemes initiated and implemented successfully by state governments. This incomplete list features creativity in federalism.

1. Mid-day meal

The concept of providing free meals to children in schools was started as early as in the 1920s by the Madras Corporation Council, under President P. Theagaraya Chetty. In 1956, Tamil Nadu Chief Minister K.

Kamaraj decided to provide free meals to poor children in all primary schools. Chief Minister M.G. Ramachandran, or MGR, further extended the scope of mid-day meals to Anganwadis and primary schools in rural and urban areas. Years later, M. Karunanidhi introduced the concept of adding boiled eggs to the meal. The success of the scheme led to its national rollout in 1995. Today, 12 crore children in 11 lakh schools are part of the programme.

2. Kanyashree, direct benefit transfer for girls

West Bengal Chief Minister Mamata Banerjee launched Kanyashree in 2013, a direct benefit cash transfer scheme which incentivizes girls to pursue education for a longer time and put off marriage at least till they are eighteen.

Besides an annual scholarship for girl students between thirteen and eighteen years of age, a one-time grant of 25,000 rupees is paid after a girl turns eighteen, provided she is engaged in an academic or occupational pursuit and is not married. It has led to improved outcomes in the health of the girl child, her financial stability and social empowerment. The scheme has benefitted around 1 crore girl students and was awarded the Public Service Award by the United Nations in 2017.

3. Mohalla clinics

To cater to the poor and vulnerable in slums, colonies and rural areas, those who have limited or no access to primary healthcare, Delhi Chief Minister Arvind Kejriwal rolled out Mohalla clinics. These clinics aim to provide basic medical care, diagnostic tests and free medicines to communities at their doorstep. Since its inception, over 2 crore people have been treated in these clinics, averaging 65,000 to 75,000 patients per day by some estimates. This is a positive first step towards achieving universal free healthcare. The project has been lauded by former United Nations Secretary-General Kofi Annan, and by former Director-General of the World Health Organization (WHO) Gro Harlem Brundtland.

4. AMMA CANTEEN

Officially called 'Amma Unavagam', these budget restaurants were launched in 2013 by Tamil Nadu Chief Minister J. Jayalalithaa. Though it was started with the aim to provide low-cost nutritious meals to the underprivileged, it became a hit amongst people from all sections of society. The canteens offer breakfast, lunch and dinner, with items like an idli for a rupee, curd rice at three rupees and sambar rice at five rupees. Not only has this slashed the food cost for lakhs of people eating there, it has also generated jobs for thousands of women who staff the canteens. During the pandemic, Amma Canteens served 11 lakh people every day.

5. SWASTHYA SATHI, HEALTH CARD

This health insurance scheme was launched by the West Bengal Chief Minister in 2016, two years before the launch of the Union government's PM-Jan Arogya Yojana (Ayushman Bharat). Swasthya Sathi provides health insurance cover up to 5 lakh rupees per annum, and is paperless, cashless and smart card-based. All pre-existing diseases are covered. There is no cap on the family size, and parents of both the husband and the wife are also covered, including any person with physical disabilities in the family. The entire premium is borne by the state government and no contribution is needed from the beneficiary. To encourage women's empowerment, the smart card is in the name of the female head of the family. There are 2,200 empanelled hospitals and the scheme covers 2.5 crore families in the state, with a claim settlement rate of 98%.[166]

6. FREE BICYCLES FOR GIRL STUDENTS

The brainchild of Bihar Chief Minister Nitish Kumar—the Mukhyamantri Balika Cycle Yojana of 2006 entitles girls in ninth and tenth standards to a free cycle, or one at the cost of 2,000 rupees. The impact of the scheme was evident when the number of girls registered in ninth standard in state government schools more than tripled in four years, from 1.75 lakh to 6 lakh. The drop-out rate also reduced significantly. The success of the programme led to other states adopting the concept.

There are many other schemes from states across India which have been successful. It is only by emulating innovative public policy programmes which have a proven track record in states, and implementing them nationally, that India can reap, what I call, the federalism dividend.

3

BJP's Double-Engine Sarkars Have Hurt the Poor

'My political instincts tell me that MNREGA should not be discontinued because it is a living memorial to your (Congress's) failures. After so many years in power, all you were able to deliver is for a poor man to dig ditches a few days a month.'

—Prime Minister Narendra Modi in Lok Sabha,
February 2015

The PM bad-mouthed previous governments on the floor of Parliament. But in doing so, even he has to acknowledge that Mahatma Gandhi National Rural Employment Guarantee Act (MNREGA), with over 26 crore workers on its rolls,[167] is a key economic growth driver, alleviating poverty in rural India. In Parliament, the Union government was questioned on the reduction in the budget estimate of MNREGA from 98,000 crore rupees in FY 2022 to 60,000 crore rupees in 2023.[168] The government answered that MNREGA is a demand-driven employment scheme and the ministry seeks additional funds only when it is required to meet the demand for work on the ground.

Was it the Union government's suggestion that there is a lack of demand for MNREGA in the country?

MNREGA AS A SAFETY NET

The job market is facing a major crisis, with the unemployment rate hovering around 8%.[169] MNREGA has been pivotal in providing employment opportunities to rural households, especially landless labourers, minorities and women, working as a shield against a life of penury.

The Situation Assessment Survey of Farmers reveals that 40% of Indian farmers do not consider farming to be their principal source of income and stated that they dislike farming as a profession. Farmers are more likely to transition from farming to rural non-farm (RNF) jobs to mitigate the risks associated with agriculture.[170]

DECLINE IN REAL WAGES

According to the National Sample Survey Office (NSSO), RNF employment can be classified into manufacturing, construction, wholesale and retail trade, and other services. Studies reveal that it is the construction sector which is acting as one of the major drivers of RNF employment since 2011-12. As per the Centre for Labour Research and Action, the growth rate of real wages in the construction sector between 2014-15 and 2021-22 was less than 1% per year (even negative in some years) which raises concerns about the type of employment generated within the RNF sector.[171]

NSSO further defines the type of employment that the RNF generates under three broad categories, such as self-employment, regular salaried employment and casual wage employment. In India, there has been a decline in self-employment and a gradual shift towards casual wage employment, which is non-agricultural wage labour driven by the construction sector. The transition from agricultural to non-agricultural employment aligns with the findings in the Reserve Bank of India's Handbook of Statistics of Indian States. The gradual shift in employment from wage labour in the agricultural sector to non-agricultural wage labour in rural areas is explained by the significant decline in real agricultural wages.

INSTITUTIONAL BARRIERS

A scheme such as MNREGA, which provides regular salaried employment to rural households, is a choice between starvation and work stability for landless people. Problems relating to the number of workdays going down from 100 to thirty-one days, along with poor administrative rationing of jobs among job seekers, and delays in wage payments act as institutional barriers for the rural poor.

Decisions such as using the National Monitoring System app to monitor attendance and Aadhaar-based payment system (ABPS), when nearly 11 crore (40%) workers do not possess Aadhaar-linked bank accounts, have further pushed the rural poor into extreme vulnerability.[172] However, the Union government does not even acknowledge the problem associated with ABPS. In reply to a question in Parliament, the government stated that no workers have been denied wage payment due to ABPS, and it is neither open to technical glitches nor prone to misuse.

The latest Periodic Labour Force Survey report states that agriculture continues to remain the largest employer of the rural workforce. This implies that the mobility of the workforce from the rural agrarian sector to the RNF sector has failed. Rural households often consider the RNF casual wage employment as a last resort for their survival. That is why it is essential to strengthen MNREGA, and end the perpetual cycle of casual wage employment and extreme poverty faced by workers.

ECONOMIC BLOCKADE OF STATES

One of the key schemes which relies on Union–state synergy is MNREGA. States run by non-BJP governments have been penalized by the Union government, which creates an economic blockade.

In the 2021-22 fiscal, West Bengal topped the list of states in terms of the number of people employed under the scheme (over 1 crore) and in terms of person days generated (36 crore). However, funds to the state have been stopped by the Union government under extended imposition of Section 27 of MNREGA since December 2021. This, in spite of all compliances being met.

The Union government owes Bengal a whopping 6,913 crore rupees under MNREGA.[173] Data tabled in Parliament reveals the drastic fall in employment since the embargo of funds—the number of person days generated has shrunk to 3 crore, one-twelfth of what it was. Unfairly stopping wages leads to victimization of workers and may push them to the brink of starvation. The state government has been funding the scheme from its own budget for the rural poor. Persons with job cards have also been subsumed into work under state government schemes.

The Union government has also withheld over 8,140 crore rupees owed to Bengal under the PM Awas Yojana (Grameen); over 11,36,000 families have been deprived of housing benefits.

Letters and countless reminders failed. A contingent of MPs and other ministers from the state observed a satyagraha at Delhi's Raj Ghat in October 2023. Rightful wages under MNREGA have been denied to 59 crore workers in Bengal. Is anybody listening?

4

What the Union Government Can Learn from States: How Direct Benefit Transfer Empowers Women

Let me begin by sharing a few startling statistics: India's female labour force participation rate is just 28%.[174] One out of three young people is not engaged in education, employment or training, with women making up 95% of this group.[175] For every five men in managerial positions, only one is a woman.[176] India ranked 131st out of 148 countries in the Global Gender Gap Index 2025, a two-place drop from the previous year.[177] Three out of ten women in the age group of 18–49 years have experienced violence from their spouses as per a survey by NITI Aayog.[178]

In election manifestos, speeches in Parliament or internal resolutions, every political party will tell you that there is *a need for women to be empowered, financially and socially*. That is easier said than done. The challenge is: how do you provide financial autonomy, or even a small degree of financial autonomy, when the majority of women are outside the purview of the labour force? Enter, Direct Benefit Transfers (DBT).

All the ground research data that I have gleaned on this subject indicates one important trend: much of the income that comes through

DBT is spent by the woman at her own discretion. Targeting low-income households through these schemes is especially beneficial as these households allocate a larger proportion of their income to basic necessities like food and fuel. This is evident from the fact that the bottom 20% of rural households spend 53% of their income on food, while urban households in the same bracket allocate 49%. Given these patterns of high consumption, much of the money provided through DBT circulates back into the economy.

Now, to the politics of DBT—which is not so cut and dried. Rolling out the scheme does not guarantee an election win. Yuvajana Shramika Rythu Congress Party's (YSRCP) Jagananna Amma Vodi, launched in January 2020, did not do the magic for Jagan Mohan Reddy in Andhra Pradesh in June 2024. In Telangana, the story was different. Kalvakuntla Taraka Rama Rao's Bharat Rashtra Samithi (BRS) must be ruing the fact that they didn't have a similar DBT scheme in place. Congress's Mahalakshmi Scheme, adapted from their own Karnataka (Gruha Lakshmi) model and swiftly introduced after the big Telangana Assembly win in 2023, paid rich electoral dividends in the 18th Lok Sabha election.

National Democratic Alliance (NDA) states like Maharashtra, Assam and Madhya Pradesh run similar schemes. Opposition states running DBT schemes for women are Tamil Nadu, Himachal Pradesh, Karnataka and Punjab. West Bengal has Lakshmir Bhandar. Amartya Sen's Pratichi Trust, analysing Bengal's Lakshmir Bhandar scheme, opined that cash incentives have enhanced women's ability to make financial decisions and improved their position within the family. The study stated that four out of five women spend the money at their will, and one out of ten decide how to spend the money after discussing with their husbands. Also, the women themselves reported that their position in the family improved, empowering them in earnest.

All these schemes are fully sponsored by the states. Then there are fifty-three ministries under the Union government that run 315 DBT schemes.[179] Of these, thirteen are related to the Ministry of Women and Child Development.[180] The ministry has an abysmal track record in implementing the schemes and ranks 31st in the DBT Performance Rankings.[181] Intriguingly, there is no central scheme that directly transfers financial support universally to all women, or specifically targets low-income women (the Pradhan Mantri Matru Vandana Yojana gives financial support to pregnant and lactating mothers).

In an election speech in 2024, Home Minister Amit Shah said on record, 'We [BJP] will not stop the DBT scheme [Lakshmir Bhandar]. In fact, we will raise the assistance by 100 rupees.' It isn't only Shah who is impressed. The International Monetary Fund (IMF) has called India's DBT schemes a 'logistical marvel'. So, should we wait for a national roll-out? This will, in a small way, help change for the better the statistics mentioned in the opening of this chapter.

5

One Nation One Election (ONOE) is Oh Noe!

Chetna Kumar, a well-known expert in the policy research space, said it on X like no one else can. 'It's rather amusing that One Nation, One Election abbreviates to ONOE—oh noe!'

After the Union cabinet cleared the One Nation One Election (ONOE) proposal in late 2024, legacy television channels—dutifully—complied with the BJP playbook. Distract from the real issues: unemployment, inflation, anti-federal policies, Manipur, a plummeting rupee, fuel prices not being cut despite a decline in global crude oil prices, and more.

This is very similar to when the Women's Reservation Bill was passed in 2023. The news stayed on prime time, tucking away the government's ineffectual handling of the Manipur crisis. These con jobs have a pattern. The Women's Reservation Bill can only come into effect after the Census and delimitation exercise have been completed. So, the earliest that it can happen is in 2034. The ONOE is another weapon of mass distraction!

As the eminent jurist and my colleague in Rajya Sabha, P. Chidambaram, pointed out, 'ONOE would require at least five constitutional amendments.' The High Level Committee (HLC) on ONOE, headed by a former President, recommended eighteen amendments to the Constitution and other statutes of Union Territories having Legislative Assemblies. This would require a Constitution Amendment Bill to be passed in Parliament, with a special majority (a majority of the total membership of the House and a majority of not less than two-thirds of the members of the House present and voting). Daydreaming is a popular hobby.

Under Article 368(2) of the Constitution of India, ratification by not less than half of the states will be required to carry out amendments to Article 324A to facilitate simultaneous elections of panchayats and municipalities. Similarly, in order to have a Single Electoral Roll, an amendment to Article 325 is required. To implement this amendment, ratification by not less than half of the states would be required.[182]

Here are six reasons why ONOE is antithetical to federalism:

- In March 1994, the S.R. Bommai versus Union of India case—a landmark event in safeguarding Indian federalism—strengthened the autonomy of states within the Indian polity. Thirty years later, in March 2024, the HLC submitted its report on simultaneous elections. However, the committee's composition failed to reflect the federal nature of the Constitution, as it did not include a single chief minister or representative of states.

- The Terms of Reference (ToR) of the HLC are, in themselves, conclusive proof of the government's blatant disregard for federalism. The second ToR tasks the committee with the dubious mandate to 'examine and recommend if amendments to the Constitution would require ratification by states.'[183] Any constitutional amendment to implement simultaneous polls would directly impact the tenure of state assemblies and governments. Even the Law Commission in 2018 had suggested that while such amendments might not fall strictly under the proviso to Article 368(2), the government should still seek ratification from at least half of the states as a matter of abundant caution.[184]

- A study conducted by International Development Finance Club (IDFC) Institute showed that there is a 77% possibility of voters voting for the same party at Centre and states if simultaneous elections take place.[185] The study analysed voting behaviour for four rounds of Lok Sabha elections (1999, 2004, 2009 and 2014) in states where the assembly elections coincided with the Lok Sabha elections.

- The BJP government, predictably, seeks to homogenize electoral opinion across all facets of political and personal life. As the 1960s, particularly 1962, demonstrated, simultaneous elections can sway voting behaviour, and sideline regional aspirations and state-level issues. In the 1962 General Elections, the party that won at the Union swept the simultaneous state assembly polls in Madras, Gujarat, Bihar, Andhra Pradesh and Assam.[186]

- The Election Commission has struggled with the logistical complexities of conducting multi-phase elections. The 2019 Jharkhand assembly elections were held in five phases and the 2021 West Bengal Assembly Elections were held in eight phases. The 2024 Lok Sabha elections across three states were held in seven phases, and even then, it took eleven days just to release the voter turnout data for Phase 1. And we are talking about conducting simultaneous polls!

- Why were the Maharashtra elections not announced along with elections in Haryana and Jammu and Kashmir? Here's why: the Maharashtra government announced the Ladki Bahin scheme in the budget in June 2024. The first tranche reached the bank accounts of women in August and second tranche reached beneficiaries mid-October. This timeline, naturally, was not conducive to the government's plan, and hence the elections were not announced simultaneously.

More questions. West Bengal Chief Minister Mamata Banerjee, in a detailed letter to the HLC, asked how many state assemblies' terms would need to be curtailed or extended before implementation of ONOE? And once implemented, what would happen if a state assembly or the Lok Sabha is dissolved before its five-year term? Fresh elections will be held for the remainder of the term. This, per se, is contrary to the very idea of ONOE. Oh noe!

6

An Excess of Cess

'Chief Minister Narendra Modi today accused the Centre of adopting a policy of coercive federalism and thus pushing states to a subordinate position by monopolizing all powers of financial allocations, reducing even the constitutional rights of states.'

—A media report on 16 January 2012

I distinctly remember the then Finance Minister, the affable Arun Jaitley, inviting about half a dozen fellow MPs to his room in Parliament for a hearty lunch sometime in 2015. Our gracious host wanted to celebrate the good news: the 14th Finance Commission had recommended increasing the devolution of the divisible tax pool to states from 32% to 42%.[187] We all saw this as a big win for federalism. But Jaitley's boss, the former Gujarat chief minister, had other ideas. A dirty four-letter word that damages federalism: cess.

As any undergraduate in commerce will tell you, cess is not a part of the divisible pool—that is, the money collected is not shared with state governments. A cess is a specific tax imposed by the Union government to raise funds for a designated purpose. The Union government currently levies a Goods and Services Tax (GST) compensation cess, a cess on Health and Education, Road and Infrastructure, Agriculture and Development, Swacch Bharat, and Exports and Crude Oil, among others.

Increasing Reliance on Cess

Consider this. In 2012, cess formed 7%[188] of the Union government's total tax revenues. In 2015, this rose to 9%.[189] In 2023, cess contributed to 16% of the total tax revenue.[190] From 2019–23, the Union government has collected a whopping 13 lakh crore rupees as cess. This *excludes* GST compensation cess. In the last five years, it has collected 84,000 crore rupees as cess on crude oil.[191]

The share of cess as part of the Union government's gross tax revenue has tripled, up from 6% in 2011 to 18% in 2021. This rise in cess and surcharge has inversely led to a reduction in the divisible pool of taxes. The divisible pool has shrunk from 89% of gross tax revenue in 2011 to 79% in 2021. This, despite the 10% increase in tax devolution to states as recommended by the 14th Finance Commission.[192]

Gross Mismanagement

A Comptroller and Auditor General (CAG) report exposed that in 2018-19, the Union government withheld 1 lakh crore rupees of the 2.75 lakh crore rupees collected through various cesses in the Consolidated Fund of India (CFI). Ten thousand crore rupees of the Road and Infrastructure Cess collected during the year was 'neither transferred to the related Reserve Fund nor utilized for the purpose for which the cess was collected'. More alarmingly, 1.24 lakh crore rupees collected as cess on crude oil in the last decade 'had not been transferred to the designated Reserve Fund (Oil Industry Development Board) and was retained in CFI'. The report further stated that 'non-creation/non-operation of Reserve Funds makes it difficult to ensure that cesses and levies have been utilized for the specific purposes intended by the Parliament'.[193]

The key reason for imposition of cess and surcharge is for the Union government to increase its revenue. One of the major criticisms has been its inability to increase revenue substantially, despite increasing cess. Revenue receipts have increased only marginally in the last ten years, from 8.8% of the GDP in 2014 to 9.6% of the GDP in 2024. Less than 1%.[194]

Blot on Federalism

In 2024, the CM of Karnataka wrote to eight other Chief Ministers, of both NDA-and Opposition-governed states, expressing concern that states with higher per capita Gross State Domestic Product (GSDP) were being penalized for their economic performance by receiving disproportionately lower tax allocations.

In the early 1980s, the Sarkaria Commission had recommended that cesses and surcharges should be levied for a specific purpose and for a limited time period. In 2010, the Punchhi Commission stated that 'extension of cesses and surcharges amounts to dilution of the recommendations of the Finance Commissions and deprives the States of their due share in Central tax revenue'. It further elaborated: 'We recommend that the Central Government should review all the existing cesses and surcharges with a view to bringing down their share in the gross tax revenue.'[195]

The recommendations of the Sarkaria Commission and the Punchhi Commission have been ignored. The number and quantum of cess that is levied keeps increasing. States that ideologically oppose the ruling dispensation are often deprived of their rightful dues. Seasoned Opposition MPs in the corridors of Parliament rue the reality.

TINSTAAFL (There is no such thing as a free lunch)!

PARLIAMENT

1

On the New Parliament and Government's Boycott of the Opposition

Prime Minister Narendra Modi and his team boycotted the Opposition. Yes, you read that right. From the time that it was conceived to its execution over the last few years, leading up to the inauguration ceremony, the new Parliament building was an exercise in architectonic narcissism. It could very well be called the I-Me-Myself Project.

There is no doubt, from the time the project was conceived a few years ago, to its opening on the last Sunday of May 2023, that the entire Opposition was deliberately boycotted by the Union government. At no stage—ideation, budgeting, design, implementation and even the gaudy opening—was the Opposition asked to contribute. Nor did any elected MPs (beyond a handful of Modi ultra-loyalists) have even a nanoscopic clue about what was going on, from blueprint to building.[196]

I did not watch the television coverage of the event. I saw many pictures on X and Instagram though.

Where was the President of the Republic of India? Where was the Vice President of India, who is also the Chairman and Presiding Officer of the Rajya Sabha? How many women? How many elected MPs from Lok Sabha? How many members from Rajya Sabha?

A few other thoughts on the subject:

1. Was there a need for a new Parliament building?

There can be two sides to the argument about whether the world's largest democracy needed a new address for its MPs. The older Indian Parliament was a ninety-three-year-old building. The Capitol Building in the United States was built in 1800, and the Palace of Westminster in the United Kingdom was last rebuilt in 1870. The French National Assembly, Palais Bourbon, was renovated during the 1840s. But was there a need to junk the old for a whole new building in India?

2. Opposition Unity

Twenty Opposition parties, in a rock-solid display of unity, spoke the same language. The Opposition had three options:

(i) Attend the ceremony and shout slogans—that would have been deemed inappropriate.

(ii) Attend the opening and then be accused of supporting the sacrilege of democracy.

(iii) Register strong protest with a concerted boycott of the proceedings, a ploy followed by freedom fighters against the autocratic British. In the end, boycott it was.

3. Intimidating atmosphere

Earlier, when the Chairman of the Rajya Sabha used to enter the House at 11 a.m., he would be greeted by MPs in different languages—from Namaskar, to Nomoshkar, to Vanakkam. All that has changed in the last few years. Now, a pleasant exchange of greetings is often drowned out by slogans from the Treasury Benches. Some MPs from the Opposition respond with a slogan coined by Netaji Subhas Chandra Bose's aide Abid Hasan Safrani, 'Jai Hind'. With this background, keen observers of daily parliamentary proceedings were not surprised at the flow of events and imagery on inauguration day: religious sloganeering, bare-bodied seers, in-your-face Hindu symbolism, the absence of every Opposition MP, presiding officers reduced to playing supporting or no roles at all.

4. No country for women

The most important woman in India, a former schoolteacher from Odisha, who is now the country's First Citizen, was missing. I can't help but ask how Naveen Patnaik and Jagan Mohan Reddy felt about this misogynistic invisibilization of the President. After all, they had instructed all their MPs to attend the ceremony.[197]

5. Why on Savarkar's birthday?

Here is a list of some other days that would have been appropriate:

Dr B.R. Ambedkar's birthday, 14 April. Jawaharlal Nehru's birthday, 14 November (or would that be asking for too much?). Atal Bihari Vajpayee's birthday, 25 December. Or, 13 May to mark the first sitting of the first Lok Sabha. Or 22 July, National Flag Adoption Day. Independence Day. Mahatma Gandhi's birthday. National Unity Day (Sardar Vallabhbhai Patel's birthday), 31 October. Constitution Day, 26 November.

But Savarkar it had to be.

2

DATA PROTECTION ACT: A SYSTEMATIC WRECKAGE OF DEMOCRATIC PROCEDURE

The Digital Personal Data Protection (DPDP) Act 2023 stands out as an example of the systematic wreckage of parliamentary and democratic procedure.

A law to protect data has been due for a decade. To bring you up to speed, there was the committee on privacy by Justice A.P. Shah in 2012, followed by the K.S. Puttaswamy judgement establishing privacy as a fundamental right in 2017. Then came the committee headed by Justice B.N. Srikrishna in 2018 and a version of the Data Protection Bill for Parliament in 2019.

In 2021, a report was presented by the Joint Parliamentary Committee (of which I was a member). A year later, the Bill was withdrawn. Soon thereafter, a new Bill, the Digital Personal Data Protection Bill, 2022, was put out for public consultation. This is when the Union government usurped all rules and procedures. Let me share an example. Comments under this 'public consultation' could only be made in English and were kept private. The Standing Committee on Information Technology decided to discuss this Bill without Parliament formally referring the Bill to it. Fishy.

The committee drafted a report without consulting its own members and only shared it with them a night prior to the meeting.

Parallelly, the Union cabinet approved an unknown version of the Bill in July 2023 and surreptitiously bypassed all scrutiny. When the Monsoon Session began, there were at least three versions of the Bill 'circulating' the streets of Lutyens' Delhi. Yet again, the Union government had cocked a snook at the legislative process.

If this wasn't enough, the Act (as passed) is rife with problems. In a swoop, the Union government bestowed upon itself excessive and overreaching powers to determine what can be said, by whom and where. The government now holds the power to 'block' 'access' to any information in the 'interest of the general public'. By leaving such 'interests' undefined, it is free to place wide-ranging restrictions on content publishing and consumption. This shrinks the space for press freedom and will make more Siddique Kappans in the future.[198]

Joining the Central Bureau of Investigation (CBI) and Directorate of Enforcement (ED), in the roster of agencies that need to be independent but only do the Union government's bidding, is the new Data Protection Board (DPB). While this is technically supposed to be an autonomous data governance authority, the fact that it will be constituted entirely by the Union government ensures that its functioning will be remote-controlled. The Union government and its agencies can exempt themselves from any and all obligations of the Act, including those that penalize non-consensual processing of data.

At a time when there already exist reports of evidence being planted by state agencies into the devices of those critical of the government (think Late Father Stan Swamy), it is disturbing how these new powers could further increase violations. The DPDP Act of 2023 also kills one of the most powerful instruments of transparency available to us—the Right to Information (RTI) Act of 2005. Used often to seek information that the government refuses to provide even in Parliament, the Bill has disproportionately empowered government Public Information Officers to reject RTI applications.[199] Safe to say that the DPDP Act is barely about how data can be processed. It is yet another devious tactic to muzzle voices within the media, civil society and Parliament.

One would have assumed that the Act would at least be technically accurate. But the Act fails there as well. The decision to exclude publicly available personal data from its jurisdiction is erroneous. Technology and policy expert Nikhil Pahwa told me: 'The Indian government has created a massive national security risk by keeping publicly available personal data out of the ambit of the DPDP 2023. This robs citizens of any protections against wanton profiling and surveillance by third parties, and legalizes profiling of the kind done by a Chinese company, Zhenhua Data Information Technology, for the Chinese government, as reported in 2020.'

The DPDP Act is a piece of furtive legislation that is fundamentally flawed.

3

SEDITION LAW REPEALED? NOT BY A LONG SHOT

Spin doctors would have you believe that Section 124-A of the Indian Penal Code (IPC), also known as the sedition law, has been repealed. While in Bharatiya Nyaya Sanhita (one of the three new criminal Acts heavily criticized but eventually passed in Parliament) the term 'sedition' is gone, it has been replaced by a new, vaguely defined offence: 'endangering the sovereignty, unity, and integrity of India'. This change raises concerns about how this broad definition might be interpreted and applied.

The sedition law was enacted by the British in 1870 and was added to the IPC in order to deal with the Wahabi Movement. Ironically, the law still exists in India even though the United Kingdom, which enacted this statute in this country, abolished it in 2009. During the Indian freedom movement, this law was used to curb the voices of freedom fighters, such as Mahatma Gandhi, Bal Gangadhar Tilak and others. Now, it is used to stop journalists, professors, human rights activists and civil society members from raising their voices.

Former Chief Justice of India, N.V. Ramana, once questioned the need for laws like sedition, as they jeopardize the essence of democracy. Its use had been kept in abeyance following a Supreme Court order in May 2022. The court had given the government time to reconsider the sedition law. This was in lieu of several advocates urging the Supreme Court to strike down sedition as an offence in any form. The 22nd Law Commission Report suggested that sedition should be well defined. The Union government has decided to do the opposite of that. Following this, the Home Minister announced that sedition had been removed from the Bharatiya Nyaya Sanhita. But it was simultaneously reintroduced with a broader definition.

The sedition law, the National Security Act (NSA), and the Unlawful Activities (Prevention) Act (UAPA), have become prime instruments for stifling dissent and silencing the voices of those whose views are contrarian to the government.

Of these three laws, the NSA is the oldest, going back over 200 years. It was enacted by the British in 1818. It gives the government absolute power to detain anyone it considers a potential threat to the nation. During the protests over the CAA (Citizenship Amendment Act) and NRC (National Register of Citizens), this law made headlines when a doctor was detained by the Uttar Pradesh government for his speech at a university. Even though the Allahabad High Court released him later, saying the Act was wrongly invoked in his case, the Uttar Pradesh government never apologized to him, and he never received any compensation for his wrongful arrest.

The UAPA also dates back to the colonial period. In 1908, the Indian Criminal Law Amendment Act first defined unlawful association in order to break the back of the Indian independence movement. The 16th amendment to the Constitution in 1967 laid the foundation for the enactment of the UAPA. The Act gave overarching powers to the Union government to ban organizations.

This law has been amended several times in independent India to widen its scope and increase its potential for misuse by introducing phrases like 'public order' and 'friendly relations with the state'. It was again amended by the Union government in 2019, giving the police powers to arrest 'defaulters' without establishing that the arrested person had connections with a banned organization. This has made it easier for the government to arrest student activists, civil rights advocates, journalists and even professors, all without an iota of proof.

Some stringent provisions of the UAPA bring into question the constitutional validity of this law. A person booked under the UAPA can be detained without charge for up to 180 days. Moreover, bail under this Act is extremely difficult to obtain. Many of those accused and booked under the UAPA, and on charges of sedition, have been languishing in jail and have been denied their fundamental rights. The story of tribal rights activist, Late Father Stan Swamy, is one of the many horrors that has been well documented.

The rampant misuse of these archaic laws has increased over the years. But what about conviction? A reply by the government in the Lok Sabha revealed that only 2.2% of cases registered under the UAPA in the 2016–19 period resulted in convictions by courts.[200] According to the National Crime Records Bureau's (NCRB) figures, the number of people charged grew by 160% in the same period.[201]

Often, when a person is charged under any of these draconian laws, the process itself becomes the punishment. The legal proceedings drag on for years. They spend months and years in jail, and lose their livelihood as well as their social dignity.

These three laws are legacies of the colonial era, and were used to throttle Indian aspirations and force foreign rule down the throats of an unwilling population. These statutes are being weaponized in contemporary India. Are we back in 1923?

4

How the BJP Has Made a Mockery of Democracy

The first three days of 2024 witnessed a massive strike by truck drivers across northern and western India. Petrol pumps started running out of fuel—there was panic buying—and prices of vegetables and milk skyrocketed. The truckers and transporters were protesting one of the provisions in the Bharatiya Nyaya Sanhita. The Union home secretary finally pulled the handbrake on the provision in the Bill that called for stringent penalties in hit-and-run cases.

Cowboy legislation

This is symptomatic of a larger malaise. Legislate first, discuss later. I have often called this 'cowboy legislation'.

Take the disaster that was demonetization. Or a nation of 1.4 billion people arm-twisted into a national lockdown because of Covid-19 on a four-hour notice. Or the case of the three farm laws that were passed irresponsibly and then forced to be withdrawn because of a powerful movement protesting the laws. Or when GST was hastily implemented in 2017, despite various warnings. Thereafter, 129 amendments and 741 notifications related to GST had to be issued in five years.[202] The Data Protection Act of 2023 was passed after only fifty-two minutes and sixty-seven minutes of debate, with only nine and seven MPs taking part in the discussion in Lok Sabha and Rajya Sabha, respectively.[203] More recently, Modi and Shah's 'cowboy legislation' spirit was also reflected in the three criminal law bills which mocked parliamentary democracy.

All this recklessness impacts, more than anyone else, the marginalized.

Consider this: after five years in prison, 121 tribals accused in the 2017 Burkapal Naxal attack were acquitted by the National Investigation Agency (NIA) court, citing lack of evidence. They were able to attend court only twice during the trial, in spite of the mandatory in-person appearance.[204] As per the Prison Statistics of India Report 2021, 77% of the total prison population are undertrials.[205] Three out of five undertrial prisoners lodged across Indian prisons are from the Dalit, Adivasi and Other Backward Class (OBC) communities.[206]

This serves as a stark reminder of the systemic flaws within India's criminal justice framework which predate any proposed amendments. Two of my learned colleagues in the Home Affairs Standing Committee which examined the criminal law bills for almost three months, P. Chidambaram (Indian National Congress), N.R. Elango (Dravida Munnetra Kazhagam), and I, submitted comprehensive dissent notes. The notes red-flagged the implementation of more stringent laws that could exacerbate the current injustices.

Lack of diversity

The first draft of the three criminal law bills was made by the Ranbir Singh Committee. The committee was composed entirely of men from similar social, professional and economic backgrounds, and experience. It lacked representation from various marginalized groups, including women, Dalits, religious minorities, Adivasi, LGBTQ and persons with disabilities. The absence of diverse perspectives was a significant concern, particularly when addressing matters of such magnitude and societal impact.

Disregard for procedure and skewed stakeholder consultation

The ruling dispensation has a brute majority in the Home Affairs Standing Committee. Little wonder then, that dissent notes from Opposition MPs notwithstanding, it was nothing but a parliamentary rubber-stamping committee. Those consulted were from an extremely limited and mostly homogeneous group of stakeholders. Accomplished legal superstars like Justice U.U. Lalit, Madan Lokur and others were not called in to testify. (It must be mentioned that one of the heads of the BJP legal cell made the cut.)

The pre-legislative consultation policy of 2014 mandates a thirty-day consultation period with the general public before a law can be approved by the Union cabinet for introduction in Parliament.

This consultation process, which involves sharing the draft with the public, must be accompanied by:

(i)   Explanations for its enactment
(ii)   Financial considerations
(iii)   An evaluation of the law's potential impact

Moreover, the comments received during the consultation should be made available on the ministry's website.

In the case of these Criminal Law Bills, however, a committee was formed with its members and objectives shrouded in secrecy, shielding them from public scrutiny. There exists a notable absence of a clear and compelling rationale for why such a substantial reform was undertaken. Especially since the Home Minister himself stated in Parliament that the primary objective was to alter a few specific sections of the law.

Eliminating the Opposition

The new criminal laws were rashly amended to incorporate draconian definitions of sedition, disregard for special statutes, rape not being gender neutral, guidelines on extensive police custody and directives on who can be branded a terrorist. The Bills were passed in an almost empty House, as the government had suspended 146 Opposition MPs.[207] These MPs represented 34 crore people, 25% of India's population. Parliament has been turned into a deep, dark chamber.

We are all for reform. Who can be against reform? But in the name of reform, let us not become more repressive than the colonizers. While there is an undeniable need to reform the criminal framework reminiscent of the colonial era, the proposed criminal law Acts endorse treating citizens worse than how 'native subjects' of the Raj were treated.

5

Government versus Opposition: On Parliamentary Privilege—and All Else in Indian Politics—There are Two Sets of Rules

A privilege motion was sought against twelve MPs for supposedly disorderly conduct in 2023.[208] A Rajya Sabha MP was suspended and a privilege motion was moved against her because she allegedly recorded proceedings on her smartphone inside the House.[209] As per the Rajya Sabha bulletin published in the public domain, the Rajya Sabha Chairman had also sought a privilege motion against an MP from Aam Aadmi Party (AAP) for a bizarre reason—repeatedly submitting identical notices![210]

What is a privilege motion? The Constitution guarantees for certain privileges (rights/immunities) to both Houses of Parliament and their members, to allow them to discharge their functions efficiently. When any of these rights/immunities are violated, it amounts to what is known as 'a breach of privilege'. Parliament has the right to punish any such breaches by moving a privilege motion.

How is a question of breach of privilege raised? In the Rajya Sabha, a question of breach of privilege can either be raised by an MP or, in the rarest of cases, by the presiding officer himself. The question can either be considered by the House or can be referred to the Committee on Privileges for examination.

It is interesting to flag that out of the seventy-nine reports of the Committee on Privileges available on the Rajya Sabha website, from 1958 to 2024, the question of privilege in seventy-five cases was raised by MPs. In only four cases did the chairperson refer the matter of his own accord. Contrast this with what happened in the month of February in 2023—the chairperson referred three questions of privilege to the committee of his own accord.

The bigger question here is, what should Opposition MPs do when their voices are stifled in Parliament? When microphones are muted, when Sansad TV is censored, when sentences and even full paragraphs from speeches are expunged? When representatives of the people are not allowed to raise people's issues in Parliament, should they act like lambs to the slaughter? Or should they find innovative ways to register their protest?

Here is what two BJP stalwarts and legendary parliamentarians had to say on the subject.

Sushma Swaraj: 'Not allowing Parliament to function is also a form of democracy, like any other form.'[211]

Arun Jaitley: 'There are occasions when obstruction in Parliament brings greater benefits to the country. Our strategy does not permit us to allow the government to use Parliament without being held accountable.'[212]

As per earlier reports (2009 and 2014) of the Committee on Privileges, 'disruptions' do not fall under the purview of parliamentary privileges. The committee found that the intention of the members disrupting was not to prevent any other member from speaking or to question the authority of the chair. It was, in fact, to express their discontent over a particular issue in which their opinion was not being heeded by the Union government.

Now, let me address the issue of an MP (they could be from the Opposition or Treasury benches) resubmitting identical notices on consecutive days. Goodness me. Re-submission of identical notices has been a common practice, a precedent, for decades in both Houses. This is done by a member for multiple reasons. Most notices lapse after a specific period of time and it is the right of a member to resubmit her/his notice. Or, an MP may choose to repeatedly emphasize on a certain issue over a sustained period of time. Totally legit.

Members from the Opposition across the country are brazenly targeted every day by the Modi–Shah government's manoeuvring through agencies like the Central Bureau of Investigation (CBI) and/or Enforcement Directorate (ED). No one from the BJP ever is. In the same manner, members of the BJP are never subjected to inquiries by the Committee on Privileges. Ministers in the Modi government are Teflon-coated. If they weren't, why wasn't the Union Information Technology Minister served a privilege notice for shooting his mouth off when he was addressing a forum and disclosed classified information? The minister claimed that Parliament's Standing Committee on Communications and Information Technology had examined the Data Protection Bill and given it a 'big thumbs up'.[213] Every constitutional authority remained tight-lipped.

Even kindergarten Parliament knows that the proceedings of a committee shall be treated as confidential. Anyone who has access to its proceedings should not disclose any information regarding its report or any conclusions arrived at before the report has been presented to the House.

For parliamentary privileges and all else in Indian politics, there are two sets of rules. One set of rules for members of the Opposition. And a different set of rules for the party run by the two most famous members of the Gujarat Gymkhana.

6

Six Instances of Modi Government's Brazen Mockery of Parliamentary Process

Parliament is not just a new building; it is an establishment with old traditions, values, precedents and rules—it is the foundation of Indian democracy. Prime Minister Narendra Modi doesn't get that. If he did, why would he have brazenly mocked Parliament since 2014? Let me present six instances of dubious firsts that have only happened between 2014 and 2025 inside the most important, historic building of India's parliamentary democracy.

MPs denied their right to vote by 'division'

When a Bill is being passed in the Lok Sabha and Rajya Sabha, every member has the right to ask for a vote by 'division'. Even if one MP (yes, just one) stands up in her seat and says 'division', the presiding officer is duty-bound to ask for voting on the issue. This needs to be recorded electronically or on paper slips, making it distinctly different from a voice vote in which MPs express their votes (verbally) saying either 'Aye' or 'No'.

～

During the passing of the three farm laws in 2020, a voice vote was conducted in the Rajya Sabha, even though several members exercised their right and called for a 'division'—this was not granted.[214] The presiding officer (the then Vice President Venkaiah Naidu was not on the Chair) bypassed every rule and overturned every precedent. This was not an isolated incident. Members have been frequently denied a vote by 'division' in Parliament lately. On 27 July 2021, Communist Party of India (Marxist)'s Elamaram Kareem demanded a vote by 'division' on the Marine Aids to Navigation Bill.[215] On 28 July 2021, DMK's Tiruchi Siva asked for 'division' on the Juvenile Justice (Care and Protection of Children) Amendment Bill.[216] On 3 August 2021, many members demanded a vote by 'division' on the Insolvency and Bankruptcy Code (Amendment) Bill.[217] The Bills got bulldozed through, regardless; but the MPs were denied their right. Unprecedented.

RENOMINATION OF A NOMINATED MP FOR THE SAME TERM

A gentleman was appointed as a nominated member to the Rajya Sabha in 2016 (twelve members can be nominated by the President of India). Five years into his six-year term, he was declared a BJP candidate for the 2021 West Bengal elections. He resigned his nominated Rajya Sabha seat. A few weeks after losing the Assembly election, fighting on a BJP ticket, the same gentleman was re-nominated by the President back to the Rajya Sabha for the same seat that he had vacated less than three months ago. This was the first time a person had been nominated twice for the same term, while fighting an election in between.[218] Unprecedented.

Quiz question: Can you name the gentleman?

TREASURY BENCHES SHOUT SLOGANS AND DISRUPT

After the Budget Session reconvenes for its second leg, the Lok Sabha discusses the Demand for Grants for five ministries. The budgets for these are discussed in detail, while the remaining ministries are clubbed (guillotined) and voted on together. In 2023, this was passed for all ministries with no discussion. This also happened in 2004-05, 2013-14 and 2018-19,[219] but the reason for the guillotine in 2023 was inexplicable. It was not the Opposition benches, but the Treasury benches that were ringing with slogans in the Rajya Sabha, leading to the Budget Session being a washout.[220] Unprecedented.

No Deputy Speaker in Lok Sabha

Dr B.R. Ambedkar, while opposing a proposal to have the Speaker's resignation submitted to the President, stressed the importance of the Deputy Speaker's role in maintaining the Speaker's independence from the executive branch. Article 93 of the Constitution states that the Lok Sabha must select a Speaker and Deputy Speaker promptly after a government takes charge. A full five-year (2019–24) Lok Sabha term without a Deputy Speaker. Unprecedented.

As of October 2025, the 18th Lok Sabha, constituted after General Elections 2024 in June, had not elected a Deputy Speaker either.[221] The post has been vacant since 23 June 2019. Unprecedented.

Passing non-money matters in Finance Bills

Each year during the Budget Session, the Finance Bill is presented and passed. It is categorized as a Money Bill and is only voted on by the Lok Sabha, and is not sent to any committee for scrutiny. The Rajya Sabha does not vote on the Bill and cannot move any amendments to it.

This Union government has started the unholy practice of sneaking non-money related matters into the Finance Bill. This devious tactic allows such legislation to avoid parliamentary scrutiny. For instance, the Finance Bill of 2016 included provisions for amending the Reserve Bank of India Act of 1934.[222] The 2017 Finance Bill included provisions related to structural changes to existing tribunals and amendments to various acts to pave the way for the Electoral Bond Scheme.[223] And around half of the provisions in the 2018 Finance Bill were unrelated to taxation.[224] Unprecedented.

NO RAILWAY BUDGET

In 2017, another precedent was set aside by the BJP. For the first time, the Railway Budget was subsumed into the Union Budget. This had never happened before. The (separate) Railway Budget on the floor of Parliament has now been consigned to the dustbin. But then, are we surprised?

7

LET THE OPPOSITION SPEAK

Question: When Parliament does not function or is disrupted, who is the biggest beneficiary?

Answer: The government in power.

The logic is straightforward. One, the government is accountable to Parliament; two, Parliament is accountable to the people; three, when Parliament is dysfunctional, the government is not accountable to anyone!

The total time scheduled for the Monsoon Session of Parliament in 2025 was 114 hours. Here is how this time was divided between the government and the Opposition: about half the questions for Question Hour and half the number of notices for Zero Hour are filed by Opposition MPs. This adds up to about twenty-one hours for members of the Opposition to raise questions and matters of public importance. In comparison, the Union government gets about ninety-three hours out of the total 114 hours for government business and other issues. A whopping 81% of the total time.

There is a legitimate need to cut down on the hours available to the government. Allot some more time to the Opposition. Four hours must be reserved each week, in each House, to allow discussions on matters of urgent public importance. Additionally, two hours should also be reserved for a Calling Attention motion (here the MP brings a matter of urgent public importance to the relevant minister's notice, who is obligated to reply). This will give the Opposition an added six hours each week in both Lok Sabha and Rajya Sabha to raise important issues of national public importance. This would mean about 117 hours for government business and forty-nine hours for the Opposition. A much fairer system.

In recent years, several critical legislative decisions have been made without adequately hearing out the Opposition. For instance, the Farm Bills initially came as an ordinance and were not sent to the department-related Parliamentary Standing Committees or the select committee of the Rajya Sabha for scrutiny, as the Opposition had requested. Passed by voice vote in the Rajya Sabha, Opposition demands for a 'division' vote were ignored.[225] Ultimately, these laws had to be repealed.

Notably, in the 17th Lok Sabha, a total of 221 Bills were passed. More than one-third were hurried through with less than a sixty-minute discussion. Only one out of six Bills was scrutinized by committees. Even the ones that made it to the committees were handled casually. The Bharatiya Nyaya Sanhita, 2023, which proposes a sweeping overhaul of the criminal justice system with 356 amendments, along with the Bharatiya Nagrik Suraksha Sanhita and Bharatiya Sakshya Bill were all discussed in merely thirteen sittings.[226] In comparison, the Code of Criminal Procedure (Amendment) Bill, 2006, with its forty-one amendments, was scrutinized by the Home Affairs Committee over eleven sittings.[227]

Another recent issue that saw minimal participation from the Opposition was the 'discussion' on the Parliament security breach. In 2001, when Parliament was attacked, both houses of Parliament engaged in a comprehensive discussion involving the Prime Minister and the Home Minister. This inclusive dialogue demonstrated a commitment to addressing security concerns collaboratively and transparently.

However, in stark contrast, in 2023, when Parliament security was breached, 146 Opposition MPs were suspended for demanding a discussion on the subject.[228]

The Provisional Collection of Taxes Bill, 2023, was debated by only two and six members and passed in approximately twenty-one and thirty minutes in Lok Sabha and Rajya Sabha, respectively. Similarly, the Telecommunications Bill saw participation from merely four and eight members, and was passed in one hour and four minutes and within an hour in the Lok Sabha and Rajya Sabha, respectively. Many other Bills have met the same fate: the Jan Vishwas Bill, the Digital Personal Data Protection Bill, Government of NCT of Delhi (Amendment) Bill, etc.

Between September 2020 and August 2021, 113 notices were filed by MPs in the Lok Sabha for Short Duration Discussion. Only two were accepted. Not allowing notices for a debate on matters of urgent public importance is the most lethal device to muzzle the voice of the Opposition in Parliament. The presiding officers, in their wisdom, would do well to address this.

The re-allotment of time in Parliament between the government and the Opposition needs to be seriously looked at. This is not merely a procedural adjustment, but a fundamental necessity to uphold the principles of accountability and representative democracy.

8

In Parliament, Unmute the Opposition

In an age of WhatsApp videos, YouTube feeds, reels on Instagram and visual tweets (sorry, X posts), interventions made by MPs on the floor of Parliament spread very quickly. So why do MPs get outraged when words they use inside the House are 'expunged' from the records? Reason: once removed (expunged), they don't remain part of the parliamentary proceedings. That's the big issue.

Muzzling the Opposition

Rules 261 and 380 of Rajya Sabha and Lok Sabha, respectively, provide for the expunction of 'defamatory or indecent or unparliamentary or undignified' content. In the last few years, the rule has been often blatantly used to expunge content that is inconvenient or uncomfortable or offensive to the ruling dispensation. This strategy of the Union government of trying to muzzle the Opposition by deleting records reminds me of a '60s Asha Bhosle song, '*Parde mein rehne do, parda na uthao, parda jo uth gaya toh bhed khul jaega ...* (Let it stay veiled, do not remove the veil; if the veil is removed, the secret will be out ...)'

Let me share an example. On 20 July 2023, I asked the Prime Minister to speak about the situation in Manipur. Nothing more, nothing less. Expunged. I'm leaving it to the judgement of the reader to decide what was unparliamentary about the statement. Even an intern working at Parliament would know that for every ten phrases expunged from the records, nine are from those used by members of the Opposition.

What do Mallikarjun Kharge, Rahul Gandhi and Jairam Ramesh of Congress, Mahua Moitra and Santanu Sen of Trinamool Congress (TMC), Bhagwant Mann—who was an MP till March 2022—and Sanjay Singh of AAP, John Brittas and M.B. Rajesh of CPI(M), Binoy Viswam of Communist Party of India (CPI), Vaiko of Marumalarchi Dravida Munnetra Kazhagam (MDMK) and Sanjay Raut of Shiv Sena have in common? They have all had parts of their speeches expunged in recent years. Some of them for allegations in the context of investment research firm Hindenburg Research's report on the Adani Group. Some, for using words like 'censorship' and 'emergency'. Others for questioning the veracity of the Prime Minister's comments, or remarks about Opposition members not being given a fair chance to express themselves.

Observations about the External Affairs Minister's visit to Sri Lanka, comments about the role of the RSS in the freedom struggle, the wide discretion given to the police under the Criminal Procedure Bill, questions about inaction during the Delhi riots, suggestions on ensuring subsidies to farmers and making adjustments to the Budget are a few other instances where remarks by MPs have been expunged.

There have been multiple instances where members are not even given notice of any expunction from their speech, and the opportunity to respond to it. It was CPI(M) General Secretary and former MP Sitaram Yechury who once questioned why an important part of his speech was expunged: 'Is it only because I used words critical of the ruling party?'

Unparliamentary Words

A list of unparliamentary words was released as early as 1954.[229] It contained around 163 words. Since they were listed alphabetically, the first word was 'amusement' (maybe you can figure out why this is unparliamentary. I have no clue!). In 2022, the Lok Sabha Secretariat issued a booklet of unparliamentary words and expressions which ran into about fifty pages.[230] This list included commonly used words such as ashamed, abused, betrayed, corrupt, drama, hypocrisy and incompetent. Some were as benign as foolish, fudge or lollipop. A close perusal of the above-mentioned list makes it apparent that the recent additions include words and phrases that have been explicitly used in recent years by members of the Opposition to describe the Union government. The power to expunge speeches is too broad and has been often used to mute legitimate criticism of the government.

PARLIAMENT BELONGS TO THE OPPOSITION

The Rajya Sabha Secretariat publication 'Role of the Leader of the House, Leader of the Opposition and Whips' quotes the 1969 book *Cabinet Government*: 'Attacks upon the government and individual ministers are the functions of the Opposition. The duty of the Opposition is to oppose. That duty is the major check upon corruption and defective administration. It is also the means by which individual injustices are prevented. This duty is hardly less important than that of the government.'[231] We might do well to remember Dr B.R. Ambedkar's words in the Constituent Assembly debates where he said Parliament belongs to the Opposition.

Postscript: Since 1956, the word 'Godse' has been banned in Parliament. Curiously, the word was reinstated in 2015. The reason? Hemant Tukaram Godse, a Shiv Sena MP from Nashik, had contended that his surname being struck off the records was unfair. The Chair passed an order in Lok Sabha that 'The name "Godse" as a surname per se cannot be said to be unparliamentary. Only in reference to "Nathuram Godse" would it be so.'

9

In Parliament, NDA May Well Be 'No Data Available'

Parliamentary questions rarely make the headlines. However, questions raised and answered in Parliament are a treasure trove of information. In the last decade, Question Hour has been a good opportunity for members in the Opposition to expose the shallowness of this government and its disdain for solid data. From the hundreds of questions asked by MPs of this government, there are seven questions that make the point that the NDA (National Democratic Alliance) could very well stand for No Data Available.

1. Ministry of Social Justice and Empowerment (Manual Scavenging)

Lok Sabha's Aparupa Poddar's (Trinamool Congress) and Rajya Sabha's Md. Nadimul Haque (Trinamool Congress) asked questions regarding data on manhole cleaning robots and deaths caused due to cleaning septic tanks. Conveniently, the government claimed the absence of centralized maintenance for this information.[232] This is despite the Finance Minister's explicit mention of putting an end to manual scavenging in the Union Budget 2023. If only words could provide relief to communities in India that have experienced the highest indignities of caste since time immemorial.

2. MINISTRY OF CORPORATE AFFAIRS (CHINESE COMPANIES IN INDIA)

The response to Shyam Yadav Singh's (Bahujan Samaj Party) question on Chinese companies operating in India in the space of providing loans through apps was bewildering. The answer revealed that fifty-three Chinese companies have established a place of business in India. But the government has 'no data available' on the details of their business activities.[233]

3. MINISTRY OF EDUCATION (DISPLACEMENT OF TRIBAL STUDENTS IN MANIPUR)

In response to Lorho S. Pfoze's (Naga People's Front) December 2023 inquiry in the Lok Sabha, on tribal students displaced in the Manipur ethnic violence, the Ministry of Education sidestepped the crucial issue of rehabilitation. In response to an earlier question in August 2023 by Dola Sen (Trinamool Congress) in Rajya Sabha, the government had replied that 'a total of 14,763 school-going children have been displaced due to the current Manipur situation.'[234]

The Prime Minister in 2016 was lauded for his statement: 'It is my conviction to bring the Northeast at par with other developed regions of the country.'[235] These words seem hollow when the students—perhaps the most affected by the ethnic strife—are the least of the government's priorities. The ministry responded with a plan for online education for students missing out on crucial years of their development. Internet shutdowns, people.

4. MINISTRY OF FINANCE (LOAN RECOVERY)

S. Venkatesan (CPI[M]) asked a pointed question on the quantum of loans written off and the corresponding debt recovery from bad loans spanning the financial years 2014-15 to 2022-23. In response, the ministry said that public sector banks have written off a colossal amount of 10.4 lakh crore rupees in loans while only managing to recover a mere 1.6 lakh crore rupees from these written-off loans.[236] This substantial loss of public funds demands scrutiny and fuels concerns about serious setbacks to the exchequer.

5. Ministry of Personnel, Public Grievances and Pensions (Pending RTI Appeals)

A.D. Singh (Rashtriya Janata Dal) asked a question in the Rajya Sabha on appeals under the Right to Information Act pending with the Central Information Commission and State Information Commission. The ministry robotically replied that the pendency has drastically reduced and the disposal rate increased. Ironically, no information was provided to substantiate these claims. No such attempt was even made to provide an answer about the states and a dry 'this information is with the state governments' was received in response.

6. Ministry of Railways (Kavach System in Indian Railways)

Despite 2023 having been a torrid year for the Indian Railways, with devastating accidents like the ones in Balasore, Buxar and Vishakhapatnam, questions about the Kavach safety system in trains were met with an unsatisfactory response. The pertinent question was asked by Dhiraj Prasad Sahu (Congress), K.R.N. Rajeshkumar (DMK), Digvijaya Singh (INC) and Dr Amee Yajnik (INC) in the Rajya Sabha. The answer revealed that the system has only been deployed in the South-Central Railway zone. The government did not think it necessary to provide any insight, plan or justification as to why the other zones were left without adequate safety mechanisms.

7. Ministry of Consumer Affairs, Food and Public Distribution (Cancellation of Ration Cards)

Lok Sabha MP Deepak Adhikari (Trinamool Congress) asked a question about the deletion and cancellation of fake ration cards over the past two years. The data provided revealed that Uttar Pradesh and Madhya Pradesh together accounted for a whopping 27 lakh cards, whereas West Bengal only had 6 lakh cards cancelled. One is forced to think—why were so many fake cards required in the first place?

8. Ministry of Housing and Urban Development (Homelessness)

I asked a question in Parliament about homelessness in the country. The answer by the ministry? Data from thirteen years ago. As of 2011, 17 lakh people were homeless, 9 lakh out of this population struggled in urban centres. India's population has increased by 20 crore after that. Policies made with reliance on such outdated data undermine the problem and leave Indians homeless.

Postscript: For over sixty years, Question Hour was taken up at 11 a.m., followed by Zero Hour at noon in the Rajya Sabha. Question Hour would often be disrupted due to MPs wanting to raise crucial issues at the start of the day. In 2014, former Chairman Hamid Ansari flipped the timings and now Zero Hour starts at 11 a.m., followed by Question Hour at noon. A noteworthy reform by a presiding officer. (*Reform* and *presiding* officers. Let's not say a word more!)

10

Parliament Is Being Turned into a Deep, Dark Chamber[237]

No place for disagreements

In 1987, the Chairman of the Rajya Sabha emphasized, 'Every member is entitled to express his opinion. Merely because you disagree, you cannot shut him down. Then, there will be no Parliament.'

Between 2019–2023, MPs faced suspension on multiple occasions, marking a thirteen-fold increase from the 15th Lok Sabha (2009–2014). Compare that to MPs from the ruling dispensation. Despite allegations of sexual harassment, use of toxic communal slurs on the floor of the House and enabling a security breach in Parliament, no action has been taken against any of them. No BJP MP has faced suspension since 2014.

Quality of Committees

Parliamentary committees play a vital role by taking up crucial policy matters for discussion, inviting participation from stakeholders and domain experts. Consider this. The Home Affairs Committee, while analysing the Code of Criminal Procedure (CrPC) Bill, 2006, which had forty-one amendments, organized eleven sittings. The Bharatiya Nyaya Sanhita 2023, one of the three Bills overhauling the entire criminal justice system in India, with 356 amendments (almost nine times that of the CrPC Bill) was discussed in just thirteen sittings.

Bulldozing Legislation

Former leader of the Rajya Sabha, N. Gopalaswami Ayyangar stressed in the Constituent Assembly that the purpose of a second chamber is to conduct dignified debates, delaying impulsive and hasty legislation. Significant Bills, like the 1977 Banking Service Commission Repeal Bill and the 2002 Prevention of Terrorism Bill, were passed in the Lok Sabha but rejected by the Rajya Sabha.

In the winter session of 2023, 47% of Opposition MPs were suspended for demanding a discussion and statement from the Home Minister on the Parliament security breach. As a result, the discussion on the Provisional Collection of Taxes Bill saw participation by just six members and was passed in thirty minutes. The Telecommunications Bill saw only eight members taking part in the discussion and was passed in an hour. The three critical Criminal Law Bills were passed in five hours, with the Home Minister himself speaking for an hour. Since 2019, over a hundred Bills have been passed in less than two hours.[238]

Stealth and Secrecy

Rule 69 of the Rules of Procedure and Conduct of Business in the Council of States (Rajya Sabha) states that a Bill should be circulated to MPs two days before it is taken up for consideration. Though the Chairman has discretionary power, this was a long-established practice that had become convention.

Today, secrecy reigns supreme. Take the case of the Jammu and Kashmir Reorganisation Bill, 2019, which stripped it of its statehood. The Supplementary List of Business reached the members at 11.18 a.m., while the Bill was introduced at 11.07 a.m. It was discussed and passed on the very same day.

Not House of Elders, but Council of States

The Council of States, unlike the House of Lords in the UK, was designed to genuinely deliberate and represent states and their interests. A notable instance of this occurred in 1989 when the Rajya Sabha rejected the Nagarpalika Bill passed by the Rajiv Gandhi government. The Opposition in the Rajya Sabha perceived it as a threat to the federal structure of the country.

Post 2014, there has been a paradigm shift. The Opposition has been systematically targeted, from muting microphones and blacking out live feed, to outright suspension. The principles of federalism have been trampled upon. Bills aimed at weakening state governments such as the J&K Reorganisation Bill, 2023, and the Government of NCT of Delhi (Amendment) Bill, 2023, were passed in less than half a day.[239]

In March 2016, the Prime Minister had stated in the Rajya Sabha, 'This is the Upper House. Whatever happens in this House, its impact is felt on Lok Sabha, assemblies and municipal corporations. So we should think about how to create an atmosphere by which democracy can be strengthened.'[240]

11

A Dark Time When 25% of India Was Silenced

I was suspended from Parliament on 14 December 2023, for submitting a notice demanding a statement from the Home Minister and a discussion on 'the serious breach of national security in Parliament'. Here are the facts.

At noon on 14 December, the first MP was suspended. Another 145 MPs were subsequently banned from both Houses of Parliament. To provide some perspective, consider this: across ten years of United Progressive Alliance (UPA I and UPA II), about fifty MPs were suspended from Parliament.

The 100 Members of Parliament suspended in the Lok Sabha represented nearly 15 crore people, and the forty-six MPs suspended in the Rajya Sabha represented close to 19 crore people. In other words, the voices of virtually 34 crore people (almost 25% of the population) had been silenced.

Here is a list of the 146 MPs[241] who were suspended, state-wise, and the number of voters they represented.

Assam (83 lakh voters)	Ajit Kumar Bhuyan, Abdul Khaleque, Gaurav Gogoi and Pradyut Bordoloi
Bihar (3.7 crore voters)	Alok Kumar Suman, Chandeshwar Prasad, Dileshwar Kamait, Dinesh Chandra Yadav, Dulal Chandra Goswami, Faiyaz Ahmad, Giridhari Yadav, Kaushalendra Kumar, Mahabali Singh, Manoj Kumar Jha, Mohammad Jawed, Rajiv Ranjan (alias Lalan Singh), Ram Nath Thakur, Santosh Kumar, Sunil Kumar
Chhattisgarh (1 crore voters)	Deepak Baij, Jyotsna Charandas Mahant, Phulo Devi Netam, Ranjeet Ranjan
Goa (6 lakh voters)	Francisco Sardinha
Gujarat (1.2 crore voters)	Amee Yajnik, Naranbhai J. Rathwa, Shaktisinh Gohil
Himachal Pradesh (13 lakh voters)	Pratibha Singh
Jammu and Kashmir (40 lakh voters)	Farooq Abdullah, Hasnain Masoodi and Mohammad Akbar Lone
Jharkhand (50 lakh voters)	Geeta Kora and Mahua Maji
Karnataka (1.95 crore voters)	D.K. Suresh, G.C. Chandrashekhar, Jairam Ramesh, L. Hanumanthaiah and Syed Nasir Hussain
Kerala (4.4 crore voters)	A.A. Rahim, A.M. Ariff, Adoor Prakash, Anto Antony, Benny Behanan, Binoy Viswam, Dean Kuriakose, E.T. Mohammed Basheer, Hibi Eden, Jebi Mather Hisham, John Brittas, Jose K. Mani, K. Muraleedharan, Kumbakudi Sudhakaran, M.P. Abdussamad Samadani, N.K. Premachandran, P. Sandosh Kumar,

	Rajmohan Unnithan, Ramya Haridas, Shashi Tharoor, Suresh Kodikunnil, T.N. Prathapan, Thomas Chazhikadan, V. Sivadasan and V.K. Sreekandan
Lakshadweep (55,000 voters)	Faizal P.P. Mohammed
Madhya Pradesh (47 lakh voters)	Nakul Nath and Rajmani Patel
Maharashtra (3.8 crore voters)	Amol Ramsing Kolhe, Imran Pratapgarhi, Kumar Ketkar, Rajani Ashokrao Patil, Supriya Sadanand Sule and Vandana Chavan
Rajasthan (2.2 crore voters)	K.C. Venugopal, Neeraj Dangi, Pramod Tiwari and Randeep Singh Surjewala
Odisha (14.3 lakh voters)	Saptagiri Sankar Ulaka
Puducherry (9.7 lakh voters)	V. Vaithilingam
Punjab (1.1 crore voters)	Amar Singh, Gurjeet Singh Aujla, Jasbir Singh Gill, Manish Tewari, Mohammad Sadique, Sushil Kumar Rinku
Tamil Nadu (6.5 crore voters)	A. Ganeshamurthi, A. Raja, B. Manickam Tagore, C.N. Annadurai, Dhanush M. Kumar, A. Chellakumar, Dayanidhi Maran, D.N.V. S. Senthilkumar, K. Jayakumar, Kanimozhi N.V.N. Somu, M.K. Vishnu Prasad, T. Sumathy (alias Thamizhachi Thangapandian), Tholkappiyan Thirumavalavan, Kalanidhi Veeraswamy, Ganesan Selvam, K. Subbarayan, Kani K. Navas, Kanimozhi Karunanidhi, Karti P. Chidambaram,

	M. Mohamed Abdulla, M. Shanmugam N.R. Elango, P. Velusamy, P.R. Natarajan, R. Girirajan, S. Jagathrakshakan, S. Jothimani, S. Venkatesan, S.S. Palanimanickam, Sellaperumal Ramalingam, Su. Thirunavukkarasar, Thalikkottai Rajuthevar Baalu and Vijayakumar (alias Vijay Vasanth)
Uttar Pradesh (1.5 crore voters)	Dimple Yadav, Javed Ali Khan, Kunwar Danish Ali, Ram Gopal Yadav, S.T. Hasan
West Bengal (5.7 crore voters)	Abir Ranjan Biswas, Adhir Ranjan Chowdhury, Aparupa Poddar, Asit Kumar Mal, Derek O'Brien, Kakoli Ghosh Dastidar, Kalyan Banerjee, Khalilur Rahaman, Mala Roy, Mausam Noor, Mohammed Nadimul Haque, Prakash Chik Baraik, Prasun Banerjee, Pratima Mondal, Sajda Ahmed, Samirul Islam, Santanu Sen, Satabdi Roy Banerjee, Sougata Ray, Sudip Bandyopadhyay and Sunil Kumar Mondal

12

IT'S TIME INDIA'S PARLIAMENT HAD A CALENDAR

Historically, the Indian Parliament provided ample time for preparation. The first two Lok Sabhas (1952–1962) averaged a commendable forty-seven days between the time the notice was given and the start of the session. Over the years, however, this gap has narrowed significantly. Under the current government, the average has plummeted to a seventeen-day notice for summoning sessions—one of the lowest in the history of independent India.

India's Parliament has seen this troubling trend in the last two decades. The lack of proper planning hurts the functioning of a parliamentary democracy. The diminishing lead time between the issuance of summons and the commencement of sessions is only one of the many ills that is turning Parliament into a deep, dark chamber. If schools and colleges can set up their calendars way in advance, why can't Parliament? There are multiple advantages of preparing and then announcing a calendar for Parliament with sufficient lead time. Proper lead time will ensure higher quality of outputs from Members of Parliament.

The Constitutional Gap

Unlike many other democracies, India does not have a fixed parliamentary calendar. Conventionally, Parliament meets for three sessions a year:

(i)   Budget Session (usually February–May),

(ii)   Monsoon Session (usually July–August)

(iii)   Winter Session (usually November–December).

The only constitutional requirement is that there should not be more than six months between two sessions. The gap has enabled successive governments to carve out timing for sessions to suit themselves. This selfish tactic undermines the robustness of Parliament and raises serious questions.

Can a Parliament that meets sporadically, with just two weeks' notice, be an effective amplifier to voice concerns of citizens? Can a Parliament that gives MPs insufficient time to prepare be a shining example of representative governance? Members of the Lok Sabha and the Rajya Sabha are elected not just to legislate, but also to hold the government accountable, scrutinize its actions and debate matters of national importance. These responsibilities will be fulfilled far better with a structured and predictable parliamentary calendar.

Efforts to address this issue go back many decades. In 1955, the General Purposes Committee of the Lok Sabha explored the idea of a fixed parliamentary calendar. Then again in 2002, the National Commission to Review the Working of the Constitution, emphasised the need for a minimum number of sittings. Unfortunately, these proposals have still not been implemented.

In 2019, I had introduced a Private Member's Bill in Parliament to establish a fixed calendar for parliamentary sessions and mandate a minimum of 100 sitting days annually. This aimed to enhance the functioning of Parliament by ensuring governments do not evade accountability by delaying sessions or cutting them short. A fixed schedule would allow MPs to plan their legislative and constituency responsibilities effectively, ensuring adequate time for debating and scrutinizing Bills, policies and issues of public importance. By guaranteeing at least 100 sitting days, the Bill sought to strengthen the democratic process, improve legislative efficiency, and uphold transparency and accountability in governance.

During the Constituent Assembly debates, members like K.T. Shah argued that the flexibility of not having a fixed calendar should not lead to misuse, emphasizing that Parliament must meet often to ensure proper oversight of the executive. India prides itself on being the world's largest democracy. Yet, the strength of a democracy is measured not by its size but by the effectiveness of its institutions. Parliament is the cornerstone of this system, and its proper functioning is essential for ensuring that the voices of citizens are heard and their concerns addressed.

A fixed parliamentary calendar is not just a procedural reform, it will be a big step toward restoring some measure of the dignity and purpose of this institution.

In countries like the UK and the US, Parliament and Congress have fixed session schedules. For instance, the UK House of Commons follows an annual calendar approved months in advance, ensuring MPs can prepare and balance their legislative and constituency duties.

This issue transcends political affiliations. It is about safeguarding the democratic framework and ensuring that Parliament fulfils its constitutional mandate. Seventy-five years after adopting a formal Constitution is as good a time as any to give the world's largest parliamentary democracy a calendar with a well-planned schedule, and at least 100 days of Parliament being in session.

Let's get this done.

13

Who's Afraid of Criminalizing Marital Rape?

I introduced a Private Member's Bill in 2025 to remove the provision exempting marital rape in India. Section 63 of the Bharatiya Nyaya Sanhita (BNS) continues to provide a disturbing exception for marital rape, undermining the autonomy and equality of women. This archaic exception sends a dangerous message—that a woman's right to consent is irrelevant once she enters a marriage. This exception, rooted in outdated beliefs and patriarchal systems, is not only an affront to the dignity of women but also a direct violation of a woman's constitutional rights, including personal liberty, equality and privacy. This new Private Member's Bill is aimed at plugging this loophole and ensuring that marital rape is not excluded from the purview of criminal laws.

The Origin of the Exception

The origins of the marital rape exception can be traced back to seventeenth-century England. Sir Matthew Hale's interpretation of the law proclaimed that a husband could not be guilty of raping his wife because, through marriage, the wife had consented to sexual intercourse and had no right to retract that consent.[242] The British colonial legal system did not recognize the equality of men and women.

This view persisted when the Indian Penal Code (IPC) was drafted in the nineteenth century. Subsequently, Section 63 of the BNS explicitly provides an exception to the definition of rape, stating that sexual intercourse by a man with his wife, who is over the age of eighteen, cannot be considered rape. This bizarre exception has remained, despite multiple recommendations for change. As a member of the Joint Parliamentary Committee (JPC), which (hurriedly) examined the new laws, I and other MPs, mainly belonging to Opposition parties, submitted dissent notes objecting to this provision.

The 42nd Report of the Law Commission (1971) suggested the removal of this exception.[243] In 1983, the IPC was amended to criminalize spousal rape, but only in cases where the couple was judicially separated.[244] This meant that if a couple were living apart by a court order, non-consensual sex could be considered rape. For married women living with their husbands, the broader marital rape exemption remained. International bodies like the United Nations and the Convention on the Elimination of All Forms of Discrimination Against Women (CEDAW) have consistently urged India to remove this exception, viewing it as a violation of women's rights. The Justice Verma Committee, in response to the Delhi gang rape case of 2012, also recommended the deletion of this exemption.[245] The government has other ideas—choosing misogyny over reform.

The Protection of Women from Domestic Violence Act (2005), while recognizing marital rape as a form of domestic violence, stopped short of criminalizing it. This leaves married women vulnerable to repeated assaults without any legal recourse.

Personal Liberty and the Right to Reproductive Choices

The Right to Life under Article 21 of the Constitution has been interpreted extensively by the Indian judiciary, and in its attempt, now includes the right to live with dignity, to have safe living conditions and to exercise personal liberty. This interpretation is critical when discussing the issue of marital rape. The sexual rights of a woman are a vital component of her personal liberty. The exception denies women control over their own bodies. As the courts have recognized, reproductive choices include the right to abstain from sex, use contraception or decide not to have children. Denying women this discretion within marriage exacerbates gender-based discrimination and violence.

Privacy and the Right to Personal Autonomy

The argument that marital rape should not be criminalized because it infringes on marital privacy is based on a deeply flawed understanding of both privacy and marriage. The right to privacy, enshrined under Article 21, is not just about being left alone but also about the liberty of individuals in making personal decisions, including the right to control their own bodies and sexual lives. The landmark Puttaswamy judgment on privacy recognized that decisional autonomy—whether related to sexual activity, reproductive choices, or personal relationships—are inviolable.[246] Rape, regardless of whether it occurs within a marriage, is a violation of privacy and bodily integrity.

Equality before the Law

Article 14 of the Constitution guarantees equality before the law, yet marital rape laws in India clearly discriminate against women. While rape laws recognize the rights of women in general, the exemption for husbands means that wives are denied equal protection under the law. The exception of marital rape is not only a legal anomaly—it is a profound injustice that violates a woman's constitutional rights of personal liberty, equality and dignity. The Indian state has a moral and legal obligation to protect the rights of its citizens, particularly women, and to ensure that all individuals, regardless of marital status, are entitled to equal protection under the law.

The state's failure to remove this exception only perpetuates the cycle of violence and discrimination that continues to plague women in marriage and in society. It is time for the Union government, its allies and members of the Opposition to come together to pass a law that reflects the dignity and equality of women.

14

New Lok Sabha, Same Old Habits

The essence of Parliament lies in its ability to legislate effectively. Yet, the 18th Lok Sabha set a dubious record. In its first three sessions, both Houses combined passed just four Bills. When compared to the first three sessions of Parliament since 1950, this was the lowest number of Bills passed by both Houses in the history of Parliament. Unbelievable.

The only non-budgetary Bill passed was the Bharatiya Vayuyan Vidheyak, 2024, which repealed the Aircraft Act of 1934.

The Lok Sabha also passed the Supplementary Demand for Grants (SDGs), for which a discussion was not held in the Rajya Sabha, even though five hours had been allocated for the debate. Thus, 45,000 crore rupees of additional public money was spent without even seeking suggestions from the Council of States.

Misses of Budget 2025

Five questions for the Union government:

(i) Why did the Ministry of Minority Affairs utilize just 5% of its budget estimate in 2023-24?[247]

(ii) Why were funds for LPG connections to economically challenged households slashed by 30%?[248]

(iii) Why did the PM-Kisan scheme receive no funding over Revised Estimates (RE)?[249] This, despite the Parliamentary Standing Committee recommending an increase of support to farmers from 6,000 rupees to 12,000 rupees per annum.[250]

(iv) Why did the PM Internship Scheme utilize only 20% of its funds, even after the scheme received 500% more than what was allocated over RE?[251] Why have only less than 5% of candidates been placed under this scheme?[252]

(v) The year 2024 has come and gone. When would India achieve the target of being a 5 trillion USD economy? 2035? 2036? 2037? Time for a reality check.

SUPPRESSION OF DISSENT

The blatant disregard for parliamentary norms and procedures was on full display when the report of the Joint Parliamentary Committee on Waqf was presented in early 2025. Portions of dissent notes from Opposition MPs had whitener—yes, whitener—slathered over sentences to delete them. When will this government understand that Parliamentary Committees are set up to listen to alternative views, foster bipartisan deliberation, improve legislative content and, finally, present a document with views from across the board?

15

Parliament Session: Don't Let the All-Nighters Deceive You

For two days during the Budget Session of 2025, MPs were in Parliament from 11 a.m. to 4 a.m. the next morning. Seventeen hours on the trot. Surely parliamentary democracy was all energized and in top form. Right? No. Completely wrong. Don't let the contrived all-night-long sessions deceive you.

The Statutory Resolution to the Proclamation of President's Rule in Manipur was notified on 13 February 2025. Parliament recommenced on 10 March. Why then was the discussion on Manipur held at the fag-end of the session? Why did the government avoid the subject for almost three weeks? Worse still, why in the dead of the night? And discussed for merely forty-four minutes in the Lok Sabha.

What happened in the Rajya Sabha was even more jarring. Three hours had been allotted for the discussion. The BJP used just two minutes of the seventy-five minutes that they were allotted. In fact, when the opening speaker from the BJP was just two minutes into his speech, floor leaders from his party shut him down. Indifference infinity.

Some more notes from the diary:

Voting On the Waqf Bill

While voting on the Waqf Bill in the Rajya Sabha, the Opposition ended up with ninety-five votes. If it wasn't for medical emergencies, a century might well have been scored. Jharkhand Mukti Morcha's (JMM) Shibu Soren and Mahua Majhi were advised by doctors not to travel. Sharad Pawar from the Nationalist Congress Party (SP) and Subrata Bakshi from the All India Trinamool Congress (AITC) were also absent for the same reason. Also, one vote from the Opposition was declared invalid due to a technicality.

No Notice from the Opposition Accepted

Not a single notice raised by the Opposition was accepted for discussion. The last time a notice from an Opposition MP was admitted in the Rajya Sabha was in December 2023, when I had raised the discussion on the economic situation in the country.

Another important parliamentary device used by MPs in the Opposition to hold the government accountable is a Calling Attention Motion, which 'allows an MP to draw a minister's attention to a matter of urgent public importance'. The last Calling Attention was accepted in July 2024, on the floods in Kerala. Opposition parties pushed for discussion on issues like duplication of voter IDs and youth unemployment, amongst others. The government looked the other way.

The Opposition's New Tactic

When being deprived of time to speak or when not being allowed to raise issues, the Opposition developed a new tactic. Prolonged protests were replaced with short walkouts—these invariably lasted for about ten to thirty minutes. The point was made and the MPs trooped back into the House to participate. Walk out and walk back in. I remember this tactic from the late Sitaram Yechury's playbook.

The PM's Vote

PM Modi was abroad when voting took place on the Waqf Bill. History will record that he did not support the Bill. Or oppose it. Or abstain.

Who Captained The BJP?

The Home Minister was the government's headliner during the session. He piloted three Bills from his ministry and also spoke for forty-five minutes on Waqf, which he did not pilot. Amit Shah was BJP's batsman, bowler and fielder. For a change, he was also seen more than once in the cafeteria, interacting with MPs from different parties. Interesting times. As a colleague observed, is it the 240-effect? Or could it be a fifty-two-year-old bachelor captaining a very large state? Keen contest.

16

AM I INDIAN ENOUGH?

Many of us have never had to ask ourselves this question. And maybe that's the privilege we need to confront first. Because, for millions of Indians, especially those from our minority and marginalized communities, this is not a rhetorical question. It's a lived reality. It is a quiet burden. It is a deep suspicion cast on their belonging. Their being. Every legislation. Every policy.

The Waqf Amendment Bill, 2024, was ironically named 'Umeed'. Are we making legislation for the greater good or for cynical pigeon-holing? All this is not just about land or law. It is about dignity. About whether our Constitution still holds meaning for *all* of us, or only for some of us.

FIVE-YEAR CRITERIA

The Bill introduced a five-year requirement of practising Islam before someone can create a Waqf. This is not only arbitrary but also deeply discriminatory. No such restriction exists for other religious endowments (Violation of Right to Equality). A Hindu, Christian or Sikh can donate property to their religious institutions at any time. Why, and how, should Muslims alone prove the longevity of their faith before making a charitable endowment?

Removal of 'Waqf by User'

Another serious issue with the Bill was the removal of 'Waqf by user', a concept that allowed property that has been used for religious or charitable purposes for a long time to be considered Waqf even without formal documentation. Similar concepts exist and are protected under laws governing Hindu temples and Christian institutions. For example, the Tamil Nadu Hindu Religious and Charitable Endowments Act, 1959, recognizes temples that have been functional for long, even in the absence of formal deeds.

By stripping Muslim institutions of this same recognition, the government is creating a legal hierarchy among religious communities. This is a clear violation of Article 14 of the Constitution, which guarantees equality before the law.

Waqf-alal-aulad

Waqf-alal-aulad, created through a written deed, permanently dedicates property for charitable purposes while initially benefiting family members. It is not inheritable. The government's move to let descendants claim ownership contradicts the core principle of Waqf and creates confusion in inheritance law, especially affecting women's rights already protected under Muslim law. Such interference undermines both legal clarity and religious tradition.

Composition of Waqf Boards

The Bill changed the composition of the Central Waqf Council and State Waqf Boards to allow a majority of non-Muslim members. For instance, up to twelve of twenty-two members of the Central Waqf Council can now be non-Muslims. Unprecedented. Waqf Boards are meant to administer Islamic charitable endowments. Placing control of these institutions in the hands of individuals who do not belong to the faith defeats the purpose of Articles 25 and 26, which ensure that religious denominations manage their own institutions.

Moreover, the Bill shifted the selection process from election to nomination, giving the government undue power to appoint board members. This transformation of Waqf Boards into government-controlled bodies undermines their autonomy and invites majoritarian influence over minority religious affairs.

Centralization of Power

By assigning power to a Designated Officer (a government employee) to declare whether a property is Waqf or not, the Bill empowered the state to act as judge, jury and plaintiff. This violates the principle of natural justice: no one should be a judge in their own cause.

Further, by removing the finality of Waqf Tribunal decisions, it opened up endless litigation, weakening Waqf Boards and creating bureaucratic hurdles. It undermines Articles 25 and 26.

Application of Limitation Act

A particularly alarming change was the application of the Limitation Act, 1963, to Waqf properties. Previously, Waqf land had certain protections, recognizing that religious endowments are perpetual and cannot be claimed through adverse possession. The new amendment removed these protections, allowing those who have illegally occupied Waqf land to potentially gain legal ownership if they hold it long enough.

This provision also reduced the penalty for encroachment from imprisonment to a mere fine and made the offence bailable, making it easier for powerful entities to grab Waqf land without serious consequences. This erodes the very idea of a Waqf being a permanent charitable dedication.

ATTACK ON FEDERALISM

Land is a State Subject under List II of the Seventh Schedule of the Constitution. Tomorrow, what stops the Union government from taking over Hindu temple boards? Or church-managed lands? This isn't about reform. This is about control. And such overreach is a direct assault on Indian federalism.

WHY MUST SOME PROVE THEY BELONG?

The Waqf Act, 2025, is currently under scrutiny in the Supreme Court due to multiple petitions challenging its constitutional validity. It is a mirror. And what we see in it should disturb all of us. If rights can be rewritten for one religion, they can be rewritten for all.

This Bill violates equality. It violates personal autonomy. It violates federalism. And, more than anything, it violates the idea that our great nation is built on.

Who gets to decide how much is enough? Enough to practice our faith without suspicion? Enough to exist without having to prove our belonging every single day?

The Constitution does not ask how much we belong. It guarantees that we do.

17

A List of Laws That Need to Be Repealed

When Parliament was reconstituted after the 2024 Lok Sabha election, I had drawn up a list of eight laws that should be considered by the Union government and repealed to ensure justice, equality and liberty for all citizens.

Here are four more items to that list:

- Anti-conversion laws
- Provisions for police custody in the Bharatiya Nagarik Suraksha Sanhita
- Unlawful Activities (Prevention) Act, 1967
- Bombay Prevention of Begging Act, 1959

These laws disproportionately harm marginalized communities, restrict personal freedoms and violate constitutional safeguards.

It is time for Parliament to deliberate, critically reassess and repeal these laws to uphold democratic values and protect the rights of all citizens.

Anti-Conversion Laws

Anti-conversions laws date back to the 1960s, but there have been some recent instances of these laws being passed in the states of

Gujarat, Madhya Pradesh, Uttarakhand and Uttar Pradesh. These laws undermine the fundamental rights of freedom of religion and privacy guaranteed by the Constitution under Articles 25 and 21, respectively. By requiring prior notice or state approval for conversions, these laws impose paternalistic restrictions, often leading to harassment, communal tensions and violation of individual autonomy. They disproportionately target interfaith marriages and perpetuate discriminatory stereotypes like love jihad. These laws promote a surveillance-like state over a deeply personal choice, which is antithetical to the secular and democratic ethos of our great nation.

Police Custody in Bharatiya Nagarik Suraksha Sanhita

In the new, hurriedly legislated criminal laws, the words 'otherwise than in the detention of the police' have been deleted from the section that talks about police custody. Under the previous framework, police custody was limited to fifteen days within the initial period, irrespective of the overall custody period. This limitation is a crucial safeguard against the misuse of power and custodial abuse. However, the new provision effectively allows the fifteen-day custody period to be fragmented and spread across the entire remand period. This means an individual could be repeatedly subjected to police custody at intervals throughout sixty or ninety days, depending on the gravity of the offence. This can potentially lead to prolonged and intermittent custody, increasing the risk of custodial abuse, violation of individual rights and undermining safeguards against arbitrary detention.

The Unlawful Activities (Prevention) Act, 1967

The UAPA poses a grave threat to fundamental rights and democratic freedoms in India. By criminalizing free speech and dissent, it undermines Articles 19 and 21 of the Constitution, which guarantee freedom of expression, and the right to life and liberty. The law defines 'unlawful activity' very vaguely, which allows the government to designate individuals or organizations as 'terrorists' without a fair trial. This has enabled arbitrary application of the provision in targeting activists, journalists and students. The UAPA further erodes due process by allowing property seizures and detention without charge for up to 180 days.

The law's misuse is amplified by its dismal conviction rate of only 2.8%.[253] This highlights that most individuals subjected to the UAPA endure prolonged incarceration without need for substantial evidence. This violates the right to a fair trial under Article 22, and tarnishes India's commitment to justice and equality. The UAPA, in its current form, creates a draconian environment where dissent is criminalized, and fundamental freedoms are denied to citizens.

THE BOMBAY PREVENTION OF BEGGING ACT, 1959

According to the 2011 Census, there were 4,13,670 beggars in India.[254] The Bombay Prevention of Begging Act, 1959, treats begging as a crime, using vague definitions, as found in Section 2(1), to include asking for alms or performing on streets for money. This unfairly targets the poor and informal sector workers. Provisions like Section 5, which allows the people caught begging to be detained for up to three years in overcrowded 'certified institutions', strip individuals of their dignity. Similarly, Section 11, which permits arrests without a warrant, opens the door to misuse and harassment. Instead of addressing root causes like homelessness and unemployment, the Act punishes people for their poverty. By criminalizing acts of survival, the Act violates basic rights like right to life (Article 21) and freedom of movement and expression (Article 19) while disproportionately harming the poor, violating the right to equality before the law (Article 14). It shifts focus away from the government's responsibility to address poverty, ignoring why people are forced to beg. Repealing this harsh, outdated law would allow for a more humane approach to follow, treating poverty as a social issue, and helping vulnerable communities with dignity and care.

18

How Laws Are Passed under NDA—In Silence, without Consultation

The release of the draft rules for the Digital Personal Data Protection Act, 2023, (DPDP) for public consultation, more than sixteen months after the Act was passed, restarted discussions on the importance of public participation in lawmaking, particularly for pieces of legislation that significantly impact individual rights. [255] Given its implications for privacy and digital governance, the delay in consulting the public on the implementation of the DPDP drew scrutiny.

The instance was emblematic of the broader issues surrounding the Pre-Legislative Consultation Policy (PLCP). In 2014, PLCP was formulated by the Ministry of Law and Justice. The policy is supposed to be followed by all departments and ministries before any legislative proposal is submitted for consideration. It has been a decade since the PLCP came into effect. The question is: how many legislative proposals have actually undergone public consultation, and to what extent has the policy been effectively implemented across ministries and departments? The Union government was asked a pointed question in Parliament: how many Bills had been placed in the public domain for consultation before introduction? The response from Kiren Rijiju, then Union Minister of Law and Justice, was that the ministry does not maintain any record related to compliance with respect to the PLCP. (Another example of NDA—No Data Available!)

Non-obligatory Nature of PLCP

Paragraph 11 of the PLCP allows ministries and departments significant discretion to bypass the policy's requirements if they deem public consultation to be 'not feasible' or 'undesirable'. This broad exemption creates a major loophole that undermines the very purpose of the policy. By granting government bodies the power to unilaterally decide when public input can be avoided, the provision weakens the commitment to transparency, accountability, and participatory democracy.

Such flexibility can be easily misused, leading to important legislation being passed without considering the views of those who may be affected. The ability to sidestep consultations without clearly defined criteria opens the door for arbitrary decisions, potentially resulting in laws that do not adequately reflect public needs or address stakeholder concerns. In essence, this undermines the fundamental aim of the policy: to ensure that the legislative process is inclusive, and deliberative, and that voices of citizens are heard and considered before laws are enacted.

Poor Scrutiny and Quality of Legislation

The widespread public protests and strong opposition to controversial legislation, such as the CAA–NRC Bills and the Farm Bills, are examples of hurriedly legislating without meaningful consultations with key stakeholders. Several other significant pieces of legislation, including the Right to Information (Amendment) Act, 2019, the Unlawful Activities (Prevention) Amendment Act, 2019, the Insolvency and Bankruptcy (Second Amendment) Bill, 2021, were all tabled in Parliament without any prior engagement or consultation with the public. These instances reflect a broader trend of flippant legislative procedure without adequate public input.

Even when consultations do take place under the PLCP, there is no mechanism to ensure that they are conducted in all relevant languages and are well publicized, limiting accessibility for many citizens. Here are some startling statistics. As per PRS's data from January 2022, three out of four Bills introduced in Parliament bypassed any form of prior public consultation. Also, among Bills that were subjected to consultation, more than half (a whopping 54%) did not comply with the mandated thirty-day consultation period.[256]

BEST PRACTICES

In South Africa, the Constitution requires that all proposed legislations undergo a process of public engagement before being enacted. This mandatory public involvement ensures transparency and accountability in lawmaking, with any law that does not follow the prescribed consultation process being deemed unconstitutional and struck down by the courts. The emphasis is on inclusivity, allowing citizens to actively participate in shaping the laws that govern them.

Similarly, South Korea has institutionalized public participation in the legislative process by mandating that draft bills be published in advance. The draft legislation is made available for a minimum of twenty days before being introduced in the legislature, providing ample time for citizens to review and voice their opinions.

Given the limitations of the current PLCP, there is an urgent need for meaningful reform to make public consultations a mandatory and legally enforced part of the legislative process. Without such changes, there is a serious risk that lawmaking will drift further away from the concerns and aspirations of ordinary citizens.

The practices being followed by South Africa and South Korea are good examples of embedding public participation into the lawmaking process. This not only makes governance more transparent but also lends greater legitimacy to the laws, by ensuring they are shaped by citizens. Embracing a stronger consultation framework would give India an opportunity to breathe new life into its democratic practices and rebuild public trust.

19

THE GOVERNMENT'S PARLIAMENT-OPHOBIA

In June 2024, leaders from seventeen political parties wrote to the Prime Minister urging him to call a special session of Parliament the same month.[257] Within hours of doing so, a skittish government frantically announced the dates for a regular Monsoon Session starting 21 July, seemingly turning down the demand for a special session. Normally, the lead time to announce a Parliament session (the number of days between announcement and commencement) is twenty days or less.[258] The aforementioned Monsoon Session had been announced forty-seven days in advance!

About 250 MPs from the Opposition endorsed the letter already dispatched by their party leaders to the Prime Minister.[259] The demand for a special session was first raised by Kapil Sibal, eminent jurist and independent MP, three days after the tragedy in Pahalgam. Opposition parties took the cue from there.

CONVENING PARLIAMENT SESSIONS

Let us start with the rule book. Article 85(1) of the Constitution stipulates, 'The President shall from time to time summon each House of Parliament to meet at such time and place as he thinks fit …'

The letter signed by the 250 MPs from the Opposition parties had been addressed to the Prime Minister. Yes, calling a special session is a decision the Union government takes. In practice, when MPs ask for a special session, the Ministry of Parliamentary Affairs, after assessing the situation (and accepting the need for a session), prepares a note, proposing the dates and duration. This is placed before the Cabinet Committee on Parliamentary Affairs. If the proposal is approved by the Prime Minister, the ministry then forwards it to the President, who formally approves and announces the session dates. It is another story if the government has, what could be called, 'Parliament-ophobia' (noun): a morbid fear of facing Parliament.

Precedents for Special Sessions

Even though there is no mention of a special session in the rule book, there are numerous precedents. In 1972, a sitting was convened to celebrate twenty-five years of Independence. In 1992, Parliament held a midnight session to mark fifty years of the Quit India Movement. In 1997, a special session was called to commemorate fifty years of the Republic.

Since 2014, three special sessions have been convened. One, in 2015, a two-day session, to commemorate the adoption of the Constitution in 1949. Two, in 2017, a midnight session, to introduce the Goods and Services Tax. And three, in 2023, a five-day session, to mark the inauguration of the new Parliament building. The Women's Reservation Bill was also passed during the same session.

These sessions to mark celebratory milestones are welcome. But the great halls of Parliament have to go beyond symbolism and anniversaries.

There have been the odd occasions where governments have displayed no urgency to break the routine. In 2006, over 180 people were killed in the Mumbai train bombings. Parliament waited for its next scheduled session before responding. After the 2008 Mumbai attacks, Parliament reconvened only when the pre-scheduled session resumed.

Parliament should have urgently deliberated and discussed the events that unfolded in Pahalgam, Poonch, Uri, Rajouri—and their aftermath. Here is the most convincing precedent. During the 1962 Sino-Indian War, the Leader of the Opposition, Atal Bihari Vajpayee, then a first-time Rajya Sabha MP, demanded a special session. Prime Minister Jawaharlal Nehru agreed to this request, and the session was held when the active conflict was still on: 165 members participated in the debate—an open discussion on the war and government policy.

In the last few years, many parliamentary precedents have been ignored. Just three examples:

- The position of the Deputy Speaker in Lok Sabha has been vacant since June 2019.[260]
- From seven out of ten bills being sent for scrutiny to committees, now only about two out of ten bills are subjected to the same treatment.[261]
- Opposition MPs were denied their right to electronic voting during the passage of crucial bills like the proposed farm laws.

This Union government's tendency to cock a snook at the legislature has a history. Look at the track record of the legislative assembly of Gujarat from 2001 to 2012. The state assembly, under the then CM, sat for fewer times than it did under any previous CM of Gujarat. In this period, the average number of sittings of the Gujarat assembly was less than thirty a year. Beat that!

Are we surprised that this government has all but ducked out from calling a special session? I am not surprised. But I am reminded of my civics teacher in middle school. It was he who first told me: 'The government is answerable to Parliament. Parliament is answerable to the people.' So when Parliament is sidelined, who is the government answerable to?

POLITICS

Indian Migrants and Polls: Can the Government Make Them Feel Their Votes Matter?

The Election Commission of India (ECI) circulated a letter on the institutionalization of Remote Voting Machines (RVM) to solicit the views of political parties in January 2023.

There is no doubt that the responsibility of enabling every citizen above eighteen to exercise their right to vote lies with the ECI.[262] However, any decision to jump into this uncharted territory will cause more harm than good.

Is Remote Voting System a Viable Alternative?

Normally, enrolment on the voters' list takes place on the basis of one's own address, which is the regular place of residence of the voter. RVM is expected to enable migrant voters to vote for elections in their home constituency from their alternative place of residence. This would enable citizens away from their home constituencies, due to work, education or marriage, to cast their vote on voting day.

According to the ECI, around 30 crore (as much as 30%) voters do not vote owing to several reasons.[263] The proposed new procedure was being propagated as a step towards removing barriers to bring down this number.

Let me point out a few loopholes. For one, there is a lack of a central database for migrants. The official census figures of 2011 reveal that the total number of interstate migrant workers in the country was over 4 crore.[264] The Union government does not have updated data on migrants and the next census has been delayed. Without a reliable database on migrants, how will the ECI effectively use these RVMs to target migrant voters?

There are more black holes in the proposal:

MODEL CODE OF CONDUCT

A key maxim of fair and free voting is the observation of the Model Code of Conduct (MCC). How will the ECI ensure that there are no MCC violations if RVMs are used in places outside the home state or constituency? There will be chances of manipulation of voters if polling takes place in states where elections have not been declared. In these states, implementation of MCC poses a serious problem.

CHANCES OF MISUSE

RVMs can be misused in the same way that EVMs (Electronic Voting Machines) have seen security lapses. Then there is the possibility of using coercive measures by the ruling parties of other states where elections have not been declared. Also, who would be responsible for the security of RVMs? The state government where elections are not taking place? Or the ECI? Fuzzy logic.

We all know stories of EVM machines being discovered from homes[265] and cars[266] of political leaders.

LOW VOTER TURNOUT

There are many reasons for low voter turnout, and it is impossible for RVMs to solve all these issues. There is no evidence to back the claim that RVMs can effectively increase turnout. The ECI needs to study the reasons for low voter turnout and then come up with a well-rounded approach to resolve this.

Some suggestions: create powerful communication to change the indifferent attitudes of sections of the voting population, provide improved facilities for smooth voting, ensure requisite infrastructure for specially abled persons and, above all, be seen as neutral.

CHALLENGE FOR SMALLER PARTIES

There is a strong possibility that smaller parties would be affected. The bigger parties are in a better position to run campaigns targeting migrant voters outside their constituencies or states. Smaller parties do not have the capacity to do this, possibly infringing on the tenet of free and fair polls.

By its own admission, the ECI also has to overcome administrative, legal and technological issues before making the RVM system a foolproof one. At the moment, this is seemingly just not happening.

2

WHY ARE THE BJP AND UNION GOVERNMENT SO AFRAID OF DATA?

This is how a week in October 2023 looked like:

- Arundhati Roy faced prosecution in 2023 for statements she made in 2010![267]
- Residences of forty-six journalists, editors, writers and professionals associated with the news portal NewsClick were raided.[268]

Basically, the figurative act of 'shooting the messenger' took on a frightening reality.

I still cannot figure out why Siddique Kappan had to endure over two years in jail for reporting on the Hathras rape and murder.[269] Those who express themselves or bring crucial information into the public domain by doing their jobs as journalists or writers are being stifled in this New India. This government is skittish about sharing information. Their modus operandi has been to create an information drought on all platforms—Parliament, policy think tanks, credible data sources and even their own ministries.

Let me begin by giving you an example from Parliament. In August 2023, a special session was announced. The agenda for the session was shrouded in mystery and only two working days before the commencement of the session was the agenda announced. [270] This is a parliamentary democracy, not an army operation. In an army operation, one needs secrecy, surprise and stealth. In a parliamentary democracy, one needs cooperation, collaboration and sharing of views. Even in the articulation of the agenda, the inclusion of the phrase 'not to be taken as exhaustive' casts a veil of opacity over the discourse. And true enough, an important Bill was slipped in during the special session to make it seem as though parliamentary procedure is not a chorus, but a selfish solo.

The devil is in (the lack of) data. The horrors of the second wave of Covid are etched in our collective memory. Where is the real data on deaths caused by Covid? How many doctors died during the pandemic? The country witnessed over 20 lakh deaths in 2021 alone, while the official tally was just 3.3 lakh. At least six times lower.[271] This practice has become a trend. From the undocumented plight of migrant workers to unreported farmer deaths during the protests, to the alarming incidents of mob violence—there is now an extensive blank catalogue of unavailable data.

The Narendra Modi government has a chronic case of arithmophobia, the fear of numbers. Their evasiveness when it comes to data is not about simply 'not knowing', it is often about knowing but preferring not to tell. The next census has been long overdue, with no plans on the horizon to schedule it sooner than later.[272] While it is understandable that a force majeure event like the pandemic in 2021 did not make it feasible for a nationwide exercise to be conducted, there is no rationale for the persistent delays ever since—even after we have in every other manner returned to a 'new normal'. Whatever happened to administrative feasibility when election rallies were nonchalantly held during the devastating second wave of Covid?[273] Or when currency notes were made worthless overnight?

The Union government still relies on 2011 data[274] to account for welfare eligibility, resulting in a significant chunk of the population being excluded from essential schemes. Over 15 crore people were cut off from a basic necessity, the Public Distribution System (PDS).[275] Antiquated data, if I may stretch an analogy, is like calculating strike rates for a fifty-over match based on a batsman's performance in T20! It takes you nowhere. So, when we look at the World Economic Forum's population projection of 141 crore,[276] we see a disparity of approximately 20.7 crores between the population of 2011 and 2023. The situation gets grimmer still when one realizes that the approximately 80 crore people covered under the National Food Security Act (NFSA)[277] form just 57% of India's population—well short of the 67%, as mandated by the Act.

Behind these numbers are real people. Real stories. Like fifty-something Nupur Hati from Hooghly district in Bengal, who clutches on to her laminated job card because she has not received the MNREGA wages due to her. Or Manjul Sheikh from Karnataka, who has another story of heartbreak. The lack of data about citizens is not just an administrative crisis. It is now a humanitarian one. And all that we get from this government is obfuscation. This delay in the national census, combined with vague allusions to a certain 'delimitation' exercise,[278] particularly in light of the Women's Reservation Bill, has only added to the mystery. We must not make welfare a privilege reserved for the statistically favoured.

Another important tool through which Parliament keeps the Union government in check is parliamentary questions. The Union government, in reply to countless questions, keeps admitting that it does not have any data available on multiple subjects—people who lost their jobs during the pandemic, and its adverse impact on the economy;[279] the number of journalists arrested while performing their duty;[280] deaths of Right to Information (RTI) activists and applicants;[281] among others. No Data Available for the NDA has become a worn-out joke.

3

LESS WELFARE, MORE PR

The Union government's welfare schemes are often more hype than substance. Slick marketing succeeds in hiding the flaws. Glib speeches at election rallies present these schemes as 'gifts' from the supreme captain, rather than what they are: repackaged social welfare schemes, copy-pasted from the states or rebranded programmes that predate Narendra Modi at Lok Kalyan Marg.

Let's examine some of these schemes. How effective have they been? Did they hit a glorious six? Or have they turned out to be a forgettable over of wides and no-balls?

AYUSHMAN BHARAT

In 2023, this massively publicized health insurance scheme made headlines, albeit for all the wrong reasons. The Comptroller and Auditor General (CAG), the supreme audit institution of India, pointed out glaring discrepancies in its report. About 7.5 lakh beneficiaries were linked with a single cell phone number—9999999999.[282] An amount of 1.1 crore rupees was disbursed to patients who were supposedly deceased.[283] In 2.25 lakh cases, the date of surgery was recorded after the date of discharge.[284] Health insurance fraud in the United States and Europe is estimated to be 10% of healthcare spending. In India, that number is estimated to be 35%.

BETI BACHAO BETI PADHAO[285]

Almost 80% of funds spent between 2016 and 2019 under this scheme were used solely for media campaigns and advocacy. The total budget allocation under the scheme has been only 848 crore rupees since its inception, excluding FY 2020. During this period, an amount of 622.48 crore rupees was released to the states. This works out to a measly 3.58 crore rupees per state per year.[286] A study conducted by the National Council of Applied Economic Research (NCAER) found loopholes in the implementation process and identified structural barriers to entry and retention of girls in schools. It showed that three out of four schools pointed towards the unavailability of clean functional toilets, inability to buy uniforms or books, and lack of safe commuting options as key constraints to the education of girls.

PM POSHAN

The Union Budget 2025-26 had increased allocation by just 0.26% for this social security programme for women and children. PM POSHAN received an outlay of 12,500 crore rupees in 2025. The actual expenditure for the scheme was 10,000 crore rupees in 2024-25, while the Budget allocation for the same year was 12,467 crore rupees.[287]

The National Family Health Survey (NFHS) 2019–21 report showed that one out of three children in India, under the age of five years, were stunted or had not achieved the standard height for that age group.[288] India also recorded the highest child wasting (low weight for height) rate in the world.[289] Figures from 2021 indicate that Uttar Pradesh was one of the worst performers in utilizing funds allocated for POSHAN—the Ajay Bisht government failed to utilize two-thirds of its funds.

Jan Dhan Yojana and Accident Insurance

As of 2022, over 8% of the Jan Dhan accounts were zero balance accounts;[290] 18% of the total accounts are either dormant or inoperative.[291] The number of Rupay-linked accidental insurance claim settlements (linked to Jan Dhan accounts) decreased from 1,853 in 2019 to 188 in 2022. Only 10% of claims were settled in 2022, compared to 2019.

Minority Scholarships[292]

The Maulana Azad Fellowship scheme provided to six notified minority communities—Muslim, Buddhist, Christian, Jain, Parsi and Sikh—to pursue MPhils and PhDs was discontinued in 2022.[293] This deprived thousands of research fellows from benefiting from the scheme. In the same year, the 'sab ka saath, sab ka vikas' government stopped, in part, the two-decade-old Begum Hazrat Mahal pre-matric scholarships for minorities, for classes one to eight, retaining them only for classes nine to twelve.[294] The government also slashed funding to the thirty-four-year-old Maulana Azad Education Foundation, a nonprofit that administers a variety of education and skill-based opportunities for 'educationally backward' minorities, from 90 crore rupees to 1 lakh rupees.[295] *One lakh rupees.*

Many states run by non-BJP parties have similar schemes, often started even before the Union government padded up to bat. The welfare programmes launched and implemented by these states have a better scorecard when it comes to outreach and implementation compared to what the Union government has done since 2014.

4

Gujarat Model Is Glasshouse Model

Let us look at six parameters to bust the marketing myth that is the Gujarat Model: poverty, education, health, State Public Sector Undertakings (SPSUs), public infrastructure and labour.

Poverty

As of March 2021, around one-third of the state's population—over 31 lakh families—lives below the poverty line (BPL).[296] Of them, 16 lakh are classified as extremely poor.[297] Between 2020 and 2022, over 3,100 families fell below the poverty line, while only seventeen families managed to move out of it.

Education

Over the last twenty years, Gujarat has allocated less than 2.5% of its Gross State Domestic Product (GDSP) to education.[298] This is far below the 6% allocation mandated by the National Education Policy (NEP) of 2020[299] and the Kothari Commission of 1966.[300] The prescribed pupil-teacher ratio in the state was not achieved in over 1,100 primary schools and 3,000 upper primary schools.

The percentage of children aged five years[301] who attended pre-primary school during the 2019 school year was 7% in Gujarat compared to the national average of 14%.[302] For five years straight (2012–2017), the state failed to achieve the Right to Education target.[303] While 41% women have ten or more years of schooling nationally, this is true for just 34% women in Gujarat.[304]

Health and Nutrition

Per the National Family Health Survey, or NFHS-5, Gujarat is the second highest among all major states in the number of underweight children. The percentage of children aged between six to fifty-nine months who are anaemic was at a high of 80% in Gujarat, compared to 67% nationally.

As per the same report, it was revealed that four out of ten children below the age of five were stunted (short height compared to age) in Gujarat; the national average at the time was 35%. Children below the age of five who were wasted (less weight compared to height) were 25% in Gujarat compared to 19% nationally. Children below the age of five who were underweight (less weight compared to age) was 40% in Gujarat compared to 32% nationally. Only 6% infants received proper nourishment in Gujarat, compared to the national figure of 11%.

Women aged fifteen to forty-nine years who are anaemic was 65% in Gujarat compared to 57% nationally. Only 43% mothers could access public infrastructure for childbirth, compared to the 62% in the country. The number of beds in Intensive Care Unit (ICU) wards in Gujarat's civil hospitals is less than what is prescribed by Indian Public Health standards.

State Public Sector Undertakings[305]

As of March 2022, twenty-two SPSUs had accumulated losses of 29,000 crore rupees. A CAG report revealed that of the seventy-seven SPSUs (excluding power sector in the state), net loss was reported for fifty-seven SPSUs during the four fiscal years ending 2018-19.

Therefore, return on equity was nil. The Gujarat State Electricity Corporation Limited (GSECL) has been accused of breaching the Ministry of Environment and Forests' guidelines by utilizing the amount recovered from the sale of fly ash for purposes other than those stipulated. In more than ten years, no action has been taken for the 195 items taken.

The sole business plan[306] of the Gujarat Mineral Development Corporation Limited Company was not achieved. The company had twenty-four mining leases, of which nine were non-operational. For five of these leases, the company had neither submitted an application for extension nor engaged in mining.[307]

PUBLIC INFRASTRUCTURE

The canopy at Rajkot airport collapsed during the rains in 2024. A suspension bridge in Morbi collapsed in 2022, killing at least 135 people. The Mumatpura bridge in Ahmedabad collapsed in 2021, after one of the 113 slabs of the bridge fell through. No FIR was lodged, nor any departmental action taken.

Claimed to be Gujarat's longest flyover, multiple cracks were spotted along the 'covering wall' of the ramp of the 3.5-kilometre Atal Bridge in Vadodara. This was just months after its December 2022 inauguration. The middle portion of the newly built 100-metre bridge on Mindhola River in Tapi district collapsed on 14 June 2023. Two weeks later, just forty-two days after the bridge built on the Tapi River was virtually inaugurated by Chief Minister Bhupendra Patel, cracks appeared on it.

LABOUR

In 2021, the daily wage for non-agricultural labour in rural areas in Gujarat was 239 rupees, while the national average stood at 315 rupees, as the Reserve Bank of India (RBI) reported. Gujarat ranked seventeenth among twenty states and Union Territories in terms of the average daily wage for non-agricultural labour in rural areas.[308]

In reality, the Gujarat Model is actually a Glasshouse Model. Sparkly only from the outside.

5

THE NARI SHAKTI JUMLA: SIX TIMES THE BJP FAILED WOMEN

During its tenure, the Modi government has launched a few headline-grabbing flagship schemes, ostensibly aimed at improving the lives of women in India. However, the patriarchal mindset that lies at the core of the RSS–BJP belief system has ensured that the outcomes are very different from those envisaged in the scheme documents.

A former RSS chief had once suggested that women should stay at home and look after the household, cook and clean as part of their duty. The RSS is the fountainhead of the BJP. Are women allowed in an RSS shakha?

Here are six instances when this government denigrated women, but received their due in strong resistance.

FEMALE FARMERS

In 2020, tens of thousands of women farmers—arriving in the national capital from states as distant as Chhattisgarh—gathered in makeshift camps in Delhi, and at the borders of Punjab, Haryana and Uttar Pradesh to protest the draconian farm bills. Some staged hunger strikes wearing bright yellow scarves that represented mustard fields, while others ran medical camps and soup kitchens. Amidst speeches and silent resistance, when the Supreme Court asked them to go home, the women farmers responded with a resounding No.

The stakes were high. Distant and exploitative markets had rendered them extremely vulnerable as farmers in recent years. As per the National Crime Records Bureau (NCRB), nearly 10% of farmers who committed suicide in 2022 were women.[309] Over 80% of rural women work in agriculture, but less than 13% own any land.[310]

The Women of Shaheen Bagh

Enraged by the Union government's decision to impose unconstitutional citizenship laws that discriminated against minorities, women protestors retaliated by staging a peaceful demonstration in Delhi's Shaheen Bagh. The 101-day-long protest caught the world's attention as women across religions, ages and walks of life rallied for the same cause of justice. Shaheen Bagh became a symbol of intergenerational and intersectional political dissent to protect the Constitution. Inspired by the women there, demonstrations took place across the country.

The government clamped down with violence, specifically targeting minority-dominated areas in BJP-ruled states. In the face of severe backlash that questioned their patriotism, the women of Shaheen Bagh defiantly challenged the Prime Minister to come and speak with them. Unsurprisingly, he did not.

Champion Sports Persons

The sickening story of Brij Bhushan Singh—former BJP Lok Sabha MP and ex-President of the Wrestling Federation of India (WFI)—is too well documented to bear repetition. He was present and voting when the Women's Reservation Bill was being passed in the Lok Sabha in 2023. Enough said.

Community Healthcare Workers

In 2022, 10 lakh female health workers, who tirelessly provided last-mile primary care in India's villages, were honoured with the World Health Organization Director General's Global Health Leaders Award.[311] Once the Prime Minister's tweets ceased, the workers were promptly cast into oblivion. Despite being the backbone of the nation's healthcare system, Accredited Social Health Activist (ASHA) workers continue to wait for the recognition they deserve.

In August 2020, more than 6 lakh ASHA workers from all over the country protested against the lack of protective gloves, PPE kits and masks, delayed payments since the pandemic, absence of insurance coverage and exploitative working conditions that threaten to push them on the brink of poverty.

Chief Minister Ajay Bisht, also known as Yogi Adityanath, had promised to increase the honorarium for ASHAs in Uttar Pradesh, purportedly to end the protests. Turns out, it was another jumla.

Women of Manipur

In July 2023, horrifying news broke out from Manipur. Two women had been stripped naked and were recorded by a mob of men. Women's organizations from across the country rose in solidarity, and organized protest marches and demonstrations in Imphal, Tamil Nadu, Kerala, Delhi, Goa, Bhopal and Bengaluru. Thousands of women took to the streets demanding the resignation of Home Minister Amit Shah and Manipur Chief Minister Biren Singh, urging them to take moral responsibility for the incident.

But even as Manipur burned, neither the state nor the Union government took any responsibility. By November 2024, over 260 lives were lost and more than 60,000 people displaced in Manipur, as per government records.[312] The much-touted double-engine sarkar miserably failed to control the violent situation in the state. The Prime

Minister did not visit the state. Not a single question on the issue was admitted and answered in Parliament.

MNREGA Workers

Despite being some of the best performers under the scheme, the wages of 59 lakh MNREGA workers from West Bengal were withheld in 2022. Women constituted more than 50% of the beneficiaries. Their access to livelihood was cut off.

MNREGA was more than just an Act; it was a guarantee, a promise by Parliament to the people of India, especially women. That promise was broken.

6

Dear BJP, You Need to Take a Hard Look in the Mirror

What does an elected representative do when he is bored with the proceedings in the assembly? Hmm … In 2023, a BJP MLA (Member of Legislative Assembly) sitting in the Tripura assembly, watched pornographic videos.[313] He wasn't the first. In 2012, three BJP MLAs in Karnataka were caught purportedly watching porn in the assembly.[314] In the Gujarat assembly, two MLAs from the same party reportedly indulged in similar misdemeanours.

Here is a motley crew of six BJP leaders who did not do their party proud.[315]

1. **Brij Bhushan Singh**[316]: The former BJP MP and ex-president of the Wrestling Federation of India was on the radar as wrestlers protested against him, alleging intimidation and sexual exploitation. Top wrestlers of the country like Sakshi Malik, Bajrang Punia and Vinesh Phogat have claimed that he has sexually assaulted women wrestlers for years. Matter brushed under the mat.

2. **Tejasvi Surya**[317]: While on a flight from Chennai to Tiruchirapalli in December 2022, the BJP MP 'accidentally' (how sweet!) opened the aircraft's emergency exit without any authorization. The flight was

delayed by two hours. Even though, in the past, passengers have been booked for similar acts, the airline refused to name the politician in their statement and only made other details public after a month.

3. **Anurag Thakur**: *'Desh ke gaddaro ko, goli maaro saalon ko!'*[318] In January 2020, ahead of the Delhi Assembly elections—and in the wake of the protests in the capital against the contentious citizenship laws proposed by the government—BJP leader Anurag Thakur addressed a rally, where he raised provocative slogans. Later, he told journalists who questioned the controversial chants that he was merely asking people what should be done with the traitors of the country, suggesting that the gathered crowds responded of their volition.

4. **Akash Vijayvargiya**[319]: A BJP MLA from Madhya Pradesh and the son of Kailash Vijayvargiya (who was also BJP's leader in-charge of Bengal), he beat up an official of the Indore Municipal Corporation in full public view with a cricket bat. The incident was caught on camera by the media. Akash Vijayvargiya later went on record to justify his actions.

5. **Ashish Mishra**[320]: Son of Union Minister Ajay Mishra, he has been accused of mowing down four farmers and a journalist during a farmers' protest in Lakhimpur Kheri in 2021. There has been no resolution. The case goes on. He has been granted interim bail. After the incident, Ajay Mishra commented during a live-streamed video that the deceased were like 'dogs barking and chasing his car'.

6. **Pragya Thakur**[321]: This former BJP MP is an accused in the 2008 Malegaon blast that killed six and injured over 101 people. She is currently out on bail. She even gave a speech where she asked the majority community to keep their knives sharp and attack those who affront their dignity. She has made hate speech her brand identity.

Life has been cushy for this crew. On the other hand, there have been numerous instances of students,[322] journalists[323] and human rights activists[324] who have been booked under draconian laws like the Unlawful Activities (Prevention) Act, Section 124-A of the Indian Penal Code (now Section 152 of BNS)—commonly known as the sedition law—and the National Security Act.[325] These have become prime instruments for stifling any sort of dissent against the Union government.

Are we surprised that India ranks seventy-nine across 142 countries on the World Justice Project's Rule of Law Index 2024? That it ranks 102 across 142 on adherence to fundamental rights, 107 across 142 on civil justice, and 98 across 142 on order and security?[326]

The 'world's largest political party' (sic)[327] would do well to take a long, hard look at itself in a mirror.

7

Calcutta Judge's Political Turn—An Arranged Love Marriage?

'I approached BJP and BJP also approached me ...'

In March 2024, a sitting Calcutta High Court judge said this on the very same day he tendered his resignation as a judge. Two days later, he joined the BJP. This is what you might as well call an arranged love marriage!

This begs serious questions:

- Should all the rulings made by this judge in 2023—targeting the government of West Bengal—have been declared null and void immediately?
- What happens to the dictum, 'Justice must not only be done, but must also be seen to be done'?
- How badly does doing preparatory politics from the Bench destroy the impartiality of an institution?

The judge in question could very well put up a (weak) defence, saying this was not the first time that this has happened.

A COUPLE OF PRECEDENTS

In 1967, prior to his retirement, former Chief Justice of India Koka Subba Rao stepped down three months early to run as an Opposition candidate against Congress's Zakir Hussain in the presidential polls. Similarly, in 1983, former Supreme Court judge Baharul Islam resigned six weeks before his retirement to contest the Lok Sabha polls as a Congress candidate from Assam's Barpeta seat. More recently, Justice Abhay Thipsay, who played a significant judicial role in the Sohrabuddin Sheikh case (where Amit Shah was one of the accused), He joined the Congress soon after retirement. Thipsay was involved in ruling on bail applications for several accused Gujarat police officers in the case.

Former Chief Justice Ranjan Gogoi occupied a seat in the Rajya Sabha as a nominated MP. The 'honourable gentleman' presided over the Ayodhya and Rafale judgments. A former staff member of the Supreme Court levelled serious sexual misconduct allegations against this 'honourable gentleman', who presided over this case himself. Sinecure?

After retirement, Justice Abdul Nazeer (the only judge on the Ayodhya bench belonging to the Muslim community) was made governor of Andhra Pradesh. Justice Ashok Bhushan, also on the Ayodhya bench, became chair of the National Company Law Appellate Tribunal. Sinecures?

Chief Justice P. Sathasivam retired from the Supreme Court in 2013. He had presided over a bench that gave significant relief to the then Home Minister of Gujarat, Amit Shah, in the custodial killing case of Tulsiram Prajapati. He was made governor of Kerala. Sinecure? Or just a coincidence?

ON PROTECTING JUDICIAL INDEPENDENCE

Some members of the Constituent Assembly had strong points of view on the dangers of undermining judicial independence and proposed measures to protect the same. During the debates, economist and advocate K.T. Shah, member from Bihar, suggested a provision to prevent former Supreme Court and high court judges from being appointed to executive offices. Shah's proposal highlighted the potential for abuse if post-retirement positions were not explicitly addressed in the Constitution. He emphasized that the growing availability of executive positions in independent India could exacerbate this issue, warranting a clear and decisive stance to maintain the separation of powers and uphold the integrity of the judiciary.

The actions of the Calcutta High Court judge delivering 'politically one-sided' judgements followed by his resignation and immediately donning the jersey of a political party undermined the very foundation of our democracy. I will refrain from mentioning the name of the retired judge, avoiding the possibility of giving undue publicity to a self-serving individual.

'Judges should be of stern stuff and tough fibre, unbending before power, economic or political, and they must uphold the core principle of the rule of law which says, "Be you ever so high, the law is above you".' These words, spoken by the Supreme Court of India in S.P. Gupta versus Union of India, epitomized the pinnacle of judicial integrity and independence.

In 1995, American academic Dennis Thompson coined the term 'institutional corruption' to explain how (parasitic) external influences had compromised the US Congress and made it systematically deviate from its proper purpose.

Closer home, in 2012, a gentleman, whose ideology I did not share, but who personified the core principles of Parliament, said, 'Pre-retirement judgements are influenced by post-retirement jobs'. Wondering what Arun Jaitley would have had to say about all this.

8

Modi Trying To Outdo RSS's Golwalkar

As of April 2024, four out of ten ministers in PM Narendra Modi's government come from the Sangh Parivar. Four out of ten governors are former pracharaks and volunteers of the RSS and its affiliates. Chief ministers and deputy CMs in eight out of the twelve BJP-ruled states are swayamsevaks.

Many officials, trained and subscribing to the Sangh ideology, currently work under various union public services.

At the time of writing, the Indian Council of Historical Research, Indian Institute of Mass Communication, Film and Television Institute of India, Indian Council of Medical Research and the Central Board of Film Certification, among others, are all manned by the BJP–RSS members or sympathizers.

Paramilitary Training

An answer to a question in the Rajya Sabha showed that the RSS has been providing paramilitary training to its members.[328] The RSS chief has publicly admitted that the Sangh is capable of raising its own military force (even faster than the State's own forces).[329] In 2016, the offspring of the RSS, the Bajrang Dal, was charged with conducting 'mock drills' with rifles.[330]

In 1935, B.S. Moonje, a former Hindu Mahasabha leader, wrote in his 'Preface to the Scheme of the Central Hindu Military Society and its Military School': 'This training is meant for qualifying and fitting our boys for the game of killing masses of men with the ambition of winning victory with the best possible casualties of dead and wounded while causing the utmost possible harm to the adversary.'[331]

Nearly ninety years since, six out of ten agreements to run Sainik Schools have been awarded to RSS sympathizers or allied organizations as of April 2024.[332] At the time of writing, two of these are run by a Sangh stalwart, who was among the sixty-eight people accused by the 2009 Liberhan Commission of leading the country 'to the brink of communal discord'.[333] The Sangh-affiliated Bhonsala Military School, run by the Central Hindu Military Education Society (which allegedly trained persons accused in the Nanded and Malegaon blasts), was also approved to operate a Sainik school.[334]

The Role of RSS in the Freedom Movement

Tomes have been written about how the RSS distanced itself from India's freedom struggle. In the 1930s, when Mahatma Gandhi launched his Dandi March, or Salt Satyagraha, K.B. Hedgewar, the founder of the RSS, announced that the organization would not participate. During the Quit India movement, the Bombay Home Department, under British administration at the time, reported, 'The Sangh has scrupulously kept itself within the law, and in particular, has refrained from taking part in the disturbances that broke out in August 1942.'

Post-Independence, the RSS has been banned thrice by the Government of India. The first instance was in 1948, following Mahatma Gandhi's assassination. While banning the RSS, Sardar Patel said, 'Undesirable and even dangerous activities have been carried out by members of the Sangh. It has been found that in several parts of the country, individual members of Rashtriya Swayamsevak Sangh have indulged in acts of violence involving arson, robbery, dacoity and murder and have collected illicit arms and ammunition.'

Why did the RSS, which gives big talk about organizational discipline otherwise, not utter a single word about China grabbing land during Narendra Modi's tenure? Or about the BJP's recruitment of corrupt leaders from Congress and other parties, and using bureaucrats to replace party men in the Cabinet?

THE BJP–RSS LINK

RSS shakhas across India increased by 111% between 2014–25.[335] According to a Hudson Institute paper titled 'Hindu Nationalist Influence in the United States, 2014–2021: The Infrastructure of Hindutva Mobilizing': 'Between 2001–2019, according to available tax returns, seven Sangh-affiliated charitable groups reportedly spent at least 158.9 million USD on their programming.' Half of this was spent between 2014 and 2019.[336] Is the RSS a registered entity? It is neither a political party, a company, nor a charitable trust. So, what is it? It collects funds worth millions from multiple, undisclosed channels. Does it pay taxes?

The current Sangh–BJP leadership belongs to a generation that was raised with a commitment to the RSS ideology—one that thrives on the polarizing writings of its founders. M.S. Golwalkar's *Bunch of Thoughts* identifies Muslims and Christians as internal threats. In his 2008 book *Jyotipunj*, Narendra Modi retells the life and times of sixteen RSS men who have inspired him. The longest piece is on Golwalkar. The invective against religious minorities that Modi spewed at an election rally in Rajasthan in April 2024—ahead of the general elections— shows that he is working tirelessly to outdo Golwalkar.

9

The Speech I Wish Prime Minister Modi Had Given in the US

Prime Minister Narendra Modi addressed lawmakers in the United States of America in 2023—a canon event; barely any other platform taken by him in the country is of equal significance. Here is the speech I wish he had delivered:

Madam Vice President,
Mr Speaker,
Majority and minority leaders of both the Houses of Congress,
Members of the Senate and of the House of Representatives,
Ladies and gentlemen,
As a representative of the world's largest democracy and an emissary of its goodwill to the world's oldest democracy, I am honoured and delighted to be speaking once again before you. For democratic republics such as India and the United States, chambers and buildings such as this one—the Houses of Congress on Capitol Hill here in Washington, D.C., and Parliament House in New Delhi—are embodiments of popular sovereignty, repositories of the people's trust, and monuments blessed with the sacredness of a church, a temple or, indeed, a mosque.

To serve here, to speak here, to just be here is as much a political act as a spiritual one.

I stand before representatives of the American people from all states and regions of your country, representing both your major parties. You have welcomed me not in my personal capacity but as the Prime Minister of a friendly country and a trusted partner. This sense of bipartisanship offers a telling lesson on how great achievements in a nation's history are achievable only if invested in by all political stakeholders—across party lines. This is what defines the enlightened national interest.

Why am I making this point? It is to emphasize that the strength of the India–US relationship today, and the outcomes and agreements that we have achieved on this visit, are a function of continuity. We have built on the work of our predecessors. In the heat and dust of politics and campaigning, it becomes difficult to appreciate or even admit this. My government has taken forward the diplomatic agenda of my predecessor's government. He, in turn, picked up the thread from his predecessor. There is a thread of continuity in the service of India, from our first Prime Minister, Jawaharlal Nehru, to the first Prime Minister from my party, Atal Bihari Vajpayee, to my predecessor, Dr Manmohan Singh, to my term in office.

I spoke here in 2016 as well. I was two years old as the Prime Minister of India. Today, I have spent more than a decade in office. The last few years have shown our world a pandemic, multiple economic crises and the devastating impact of multiple wars that are still being waged. In all this, pre-existing and long-term global issues of concern— from climate change to poverty alleviation—remain, often deprived of the attention and resources that they deserve.

In India, we have responded to these challenges with the courage and determination of our people—1.4 billion of them, 65% of whom are under the age of thirty-five. Even though unemployment remains a big challenge, the energy and grit of our young people have lifted our society. We have responded in two ways.

First, during the pandemic and the subsequent (admittedly hasty) lockdown, which was devastating for migrant workers and the middle class, we deployed tools—whether the biometric-derived Aadhaar system or the national rural employment guarantee programme—initially conceptualized by the previous government to deliver welfare benefits to our people.

Frankly, I was not always a believer in the employment guarantee programme, but now recognize it has a role. In the spirit of bipartisanship that I see here, I commit to addressing concerns about financial dues related to the guarantee programmes that have come from states run by Opposition party governments in India. Democracy is about rising above partisanship.

Second, to give a fillip to the economy, we have undertaken reforms and opened up many business sectors to greater global investment as well as spending on infrastructure. Started in 1991, this has made India an attractive economy for global investors. That continuity is what defines democracy. Representative government is not a sprint; it is a never-ending relay and at various junctures, we pass the baton from one to another.

The last decade has also taught me to have the humility to learn from mistakes. We proposed and passed three farm laws in 2020, but after legitimate protests from farmers across the country, we repealed them. Then there was demonetization announced in 2016. We soon realized that this economic misadventurism failed to meet any of its stated objectives. Indeed, what India's first Prime Minister said rings true even today, 'Let us be a little humble; let us think that the truth may not perhaps be entirely with us.'

Friends, the bipartisanship and unity across party lines that I see before me are heartwarming and yet bittersweet. The new Parliament building was inaugurated in New Delhi on 28 May 2023. Many of the Opposition parties and their MPs boycotted the event. At such a historic moment, at the opening of a Parliament building that will serve our country for the next hundred years, we hope, well after our generation is gone, this should not have happened. I am not here to point fingers. All of us must share the blame; it is a shared failure. It's a moment for me to introspect as well.

In truth, democracy is not about partisanship but about partnership. Democracies need partnerships within their societies and their polities. That is why democracies instinctively reach out to each other. That is why our two great nations have forged an unusually strong bond. This is the gift of democracy—a gift that empowers us but also humbles us—each of us, all of us, Indian and American, you and me.

May those cherished values of democracy continue to keep us inspired and keep us grounded. May our countries prosper together.

Thank you.

10

Will the Church Please Speak Up?

'The only thing necessary for the triumph of evil is for good men to do nothing.'

—Alexei Navalny, Russian Opposition leader

In my two decades in public life, including three terms in Parliament, I have written on a range of subjects, but never on the Church in India. This is a first. It needed to be written. More silence on the subject would make me complicit.

A former Provincial of a large religious congregation once told me: 'Bishops must continue to lead the Church on all spiritual issues. But is it time for the lay Catholic leaders to unite, and set the direction for the church in social and political spheres. It is time that this is debated. It is time Christians from the grassroots start openly asking direct questions of the few hundred bishops who comprise the key decision-making body of the Catholic Church in India.'

More priests and nuns, usually bound by strict rules of discipline, have also begun to speak up lately. A nun, who is a leading educationist, said: 'That the bishop's body gave the Prime Minister a platform during Christmas for a photo-op is unacceptable. I only saw videos of the PM in the media. Just platitudes, nothing on the real issues.' She added: 'They can choose to invite whomever they want, but why was not a single MP from among the twenty elected Christian MPs invited? Was that a condition laid down by Mr Modi to grace the occasion?'

Spreading festive cheer is always welcome. But now, these are the hard questions that must be asked of the Prime Minister of India, Narendra Modi. Many Christmases have gone by, now answers have to be demanded.

(i)   Why did you attempt to turn Christmas Day into 'Good Governance Day'?

(ii)   Why are you weaponizing the Foreign Contribution (Regulation) Act (FCRA) to specifically target institutions run by the Christian community?

(iii)   Why have you totally ignored the people of Manipur?

(iv)   Why are you encouraging and passing anti-conversion laws across states that violate Fundamental Rights under Articles 14, 15 and 25 of the Indian Constitution? In Arunachal Pradesh, Chhattisgarh, Gujarat, Haryana, Himachal Pradesh, Madhya Pradesh, Uttar Pradesh, Odisha, Uttarakhand, Rajasthan …

(v)   Why did you push the Waqf Bill and set the precedent for a minority against minority matrix, especially in Kerala?

(vi)   Why don't you ever say a word condemning hate speeches and crude communal slurs?

(vii)   Why have attacks on institutions run by minorities been on the rise?

(viii) Why are incidents of violence against Christians increasing?

(ix)   Why did India's National Human Rights Commission lose its United Nations accreditation twice since 2014?

(x)   Do you remember Father Stan Swamy? Sipper? Straw? Death?

In 2024, twenty Christian MPs were invited for dinner on 3 December by the bishops' body. To put it more accurately, these were not Christian MPs but elected MPs who happened to be Christians. Many MPs insisted that the meeting had to go beyond breaking bread together. There needed to be an agenda. The bishops' body then circulated, in writing, a nine-point agenda to the MPs. When news of what was discussed at the ninety-minute meeting found its way into the media, the bishops' body went into damage control mode and issued a public statement denying that any meeting had taken place. Too clever by half!

Truth be told, the meeting did take place. There was an agenda circulated as well. Some of the points raised by the MPs included: (i) Need to stop photo-ops. Christian leadership should take a stand to call out those who are not protecting the Constitution; (ii) Support the Muslim community, in principle, on the Waqf Bill, acknowledging that there may be some clauses in the Bill that are contentious in a state or two; (iii) Christian organizations being targeted and FCRA licenses being cancelled; (iv) Issues of reservation, interference in educational institutions, and repeated attacks on personnel and places of worship.

One suggestion made by this writer, who was present at that meeting, was the need to be proactive and focus on a positive narrative, rather than only be reactive to negative incidents and news. The focus could be the community's significant contribution to education, healthcare and social welfare. Here are just two among the many heartening facts: (i) Seven out of ten religious minority schools in India are helmed by the Christian community; (ii) Three out of four students studying in institutions run by Christians are non-Christians.[337]

Internationally renowned Jesuit human rights and peace activist and writer Father Cedric Prakash, speaking to this writer in turn, did not mince his words: 'The Church leadership in India seems to have missed the bus. Their hearts and ears are not listening to the cries of the millions suffering in the country—particularly the minorities. Even if they are aware of these ground realities, they seem to be totally frightened of the ruling regime to take a visible and vocal stand—just in case the powers bring out the skeletons in the cupboard. All this does not augur well for authentic Christian discipleship in today's India.'

11

Election Commission: Four Questions for India's 'Neutral' Umpire

In 2024 and 2025, few institutions across the universe were under more public scrutiny than the Election Commission of India (ECI).

Since 1950, the ECI has earned itself a reputation of being an umpire whose task is to ensure a level playing field. The phrase 'neutral umpire' is redundant, because an umpire, by definition, is meant to be neutral. Independent, non-partisan, effective, fair and efficient are adjectives that must fit snugly into the pockets of the black and white coats of the neutral umpire. But in the case of the ECI, do they?

1. Did the Appointment Process Erode Credibility?

In Anoop Baranwal versus Union of India (2023),[338] a Constitution Bench of the Supreme Court unanimously held that the selection of the Chief Election Commissioner (CEC) and the Election Commissioner (EC) would be done by a three-member committee consisting of the Prime Minister, the Leader of the Opposition and the Chief Justice of India. The ruling stated that the architects of our Constitution 'did not intend the executive exclusively calling the shots in the matter of appointments'. The court also referred to what Dr B.R. Ambedkar said in the Constitutional Assembly debates, 'the election machinery should be outside the control of the executive government'.

The Chief Election Commissioner and Other Election Commissioners Act, 2023, stated that the President will appoint the CEC and ECs on the recommendation of a Selection Committee consisting of:

1. Prime Minister as Chairperson,
2. Leader of the Opposition in Lok Sabha as member,
3. Union Cabinet Minister nominated by the Prime Minister

In effect, this gave the Union government de facto power to appoint the CEC and ECs.

A former CEC called this act 'dilution of the authority', since these changes attempted to equate the ECs with civil servants, and the 'political class cannot be disciplined by civil servants'. 'Judges are given an independent stature under the Constitution because they have to decide cases that involve the government, the Prime Minister and ministers. That kind of independence is needed for the Election Commission too. This is sending the wrong message about the independent character of the EC,' said the former CEC.[339]

2. Has the Model Code of Conduct Been Violated?

Since the Model Code of Conduct (MCC) came into force for the 2024 elections, even before the first vote was cast, 300 complaints by various political parties and 2,68,080 citizen-reported violations were filed with the ECI.[340] The complaints ranged from alleged misuse of the National Investigation Agency (NIA) in West Bengal to conspire against the BJP's political opponents, 'undue influence' through announcement of monetary benefits schemes, to multiple complaints against Prime Minister Narendra Modi seeking votes on religious grounds. The ECI responded to these complaints with a sweeping 'broadly satisfied with the compliance of the code by political parties and that campaign by various parties and candidates has remained largely clutter-free'.

3. Morbi Bridge Tragedy Left Unanswered Questions

In October 2022, the ECI announced the assembly elections for Himachal Pradesh. Inexplicably, the announcement for the Gujarat assembly elections was held up by a month. The reason given was that 'the gap between the tenure of two assemblies is 40 days'. The Opposition was quick to point out that in the case of the Goa and the Uttar Pradesh assembly elections, the gap was 60 days, but the elections were still clubbed together.

Critics accused the ECI of batting for the BJP. The delayed announcement gave the party's star batsman some extra time (in the slog overs) to inaugurate projects in Gujarat. The Morbi bridge tragedy, in the home state of the Prime Minister and the Home Minister, happened during this period. Was the ECI equally culpable for the Morbi tragedy by not notifying elections in order to allow the ruling party to hurriedly inaugurate projects before the MCC set in?

4. Major Change to Rules of the Game

Let me share a specific example. In 2019, the ECI tweaked a rule related to polling agents. The rule specified that one had to be a voter of that booth or an adjoining booth to be appointed a polling agent by a political party. What was the change made? The scope was broadened so a polling agent could now be appointed if they were a resident of any booth within the entire assembly segment. Political observers have opined that this could have been done to help the BJP in states where it has a comparatively weak organizational set-up.

In 2025, the Election Commission announced a nationwide Special Intensive Revision (SIR) on a suspicious timing, just before elections, which raised serious doubts about its intent. SIR, with no statutory backing, seems like nothing more than an attempt to rob citizens, especially minorities, of their lawful voting rights. With opaque procedures and burdensome documentation requirements, SIR is a tool for disenfranchisement, not reform. The ECI, by acting as an agent of the central government, is undermining its own legitimacy and the foundation of Indian democracy.

12

No Warranty for 'Modi Ki Guarantee'

The message from Opposition parties in the run up to General Elections 2024 was a simple one: this time, it was about BJP versus Democracy. On the other flank, BJP offered 'Modi Ki Guarantee'.

Here are fifteen guarantees promised by Narendra Modi and his party. What's the warranty on each guarantee? Judge for yourself.

Jobs

The BJP had promised to create '25 crore jobs' in their 2014 manifesto. In 2023, a Union minister admitted that only '1.2 crore jobs were created since 2014'. Reportedly, the minister referred to Employees' Provident Fund Organization (EPFO) data to substantiate his claims on employment. As things stood, four out of ten graduates under the age of twenty-five were unemployed as per a 2023 report.[341]

Doubling Farmers' Income

Incomes needed to grow by 10% year-on-year from 2015 in order to double by 2022. Actual growth had been only 3.5%.[342] At these growth rates, the guarantee will only be delivered in 2035. As per the 2022 National Crime Records Bureau (NCRB) data, the grim reality is that thirty farmers committed suicide every day.

Demonetization

Bringing back black money, curbing counterfeiting, stopping terrorism, ending corruption—all guarantees have failed. Ninety-nine per cent of the demonetized currency had come back into the system. This hare-brained scheme was nothing short of an act of economic terrorism.

Ujjwala Scheme

As per reports, despite subsidies, over 1.2 crore households bought no refill cylinders at all in 2022-23. Another 1.5 crore beneficiaries bought only one refill cylinder.[343]

Bullet Train

The project was announced in 2017. Since then, the deadline had been pushed several times.[344]

Swachh Bharat Mission

In the last few years, 367 persons have died while undertaking hazardous cleaning of sewers and septic tanks.[345] This was despite the fact that manual scavenging has been banned in India since 2013.

Namami Gange

According to the 'Quantitative analysis of Microplastics along River Ganga' study by Toxics Link in 2021, of the samples tested, the highest concentration of microplastic pollutants was found in Varanasi—which also happened to be the Prime Minister's constituency.[346]

Sagarmala Project

A port-led initiative to enhance India's logistics sector. According to the Demands for Grants 2022-23 committee, out of the forty-four projects in development, thirty-one projects had reportedly not received any funds.[347]

PM Kisan

Three thousand crore rupees was transferred to 42 lakh ineligible farmers till 2021. The Union government recovered only one-tenth of the amount from fraudulent beneficiaries.[348]

Atma Nirbhar Bharat

The scheme guaranteed 3 lakh crore rupees in collateral-free automatic loans to MSMEs. However, the reality was that only existing borrowers were targeted.

Digital India

There have been several Aadhar-based data breaches in recent years. In 2023, the private data of 81 crore Indians was leaked to hackers on the dark web.[349]

Railway Infrastructure

Between 2017 and 2022, there were 244 train accidents.[350] Fifteen major accidents in 2023 alone.[351] Half of the compulsory track safety inspections remain incomplete. The Railway Budget has been subsumed under the Union Budget.

Narishakti

Until 2021, nearly 80% of Beti Bachao Beti Padhao scheme funds were spent on advertising.[352] In 2021-22, women labourers earned 60% of what men did ('Economic Growth, Structural Change, and Women's Earnings in India', CASI, University of Pennsylvania[353]). In 2022, there were 4,45,256 crimes committed against women.[354] This translated to fifty-one FIRs every hour.

Ude Desh Ka Aam Nagrik (UDAN):

Of the 774 routes awarded under the aviation scheme UDAN-3, half could not initiate operations. Of the 371 routes that did start operations, only one-third completed the three-year concession period.[355]

Hunger

Three out of four Indians could not afford a healthy balanced diet. (The State of Food Security and Nutrition in the World 2023, Food and Agriculture Organization [FAO]).[356] Pradhan Mantri Garib Kalyan Anna Yojana (PMGKAY), a scheme started in response to Covid-19, had to be extended for five more years. As the number of billionaires increased manifold, 80 crore Indians were still dependent on free rations for their meals.[357]

Modi guarantee. Zero warranty.

13

Why Voters No Longer Believe 'Modi Ki Guarantee'

12 January 2024: 'Modi's guarantee begins where expectations from others end.'

'Modi Ki Guarantee' launched as Prime Minister Narendra Modi's key campaign slogan for the general elections 2024.

14 April 2024: The BJP launched its manifesto. The cover page said, 'Modi Ki Guarantee 2024'.

27 April 2024: The day after the second phase of elections concluded, the 'Modi Ki Guarantee' slogan was put away in the closet.

In the world of marketing, a brand proposition, as the term connotes, is a promissory note—that is, a promise of substance being made for the customer, that will be fulfilled by the brand. It reiterates to consumers the key reasons to assess, reassess, buy or repurchase the brand.

Brand propositions should be conceived with great thought and care, because you should not promise more than you can deliver. As the marketing adage goes, you can get someone to buy something once, or even twice, but eventually the consumer will see through you. Brand propositions should ideally last for years—even decades.

And finally, the success of the brand lies not in the proposition itself, but in its successful delivery, in all channels of customer engagement. This means that everyone, from the worker on the factory floor, to the quality control system, to the salesman, the outlet and the after-sales service has to be focused and committed to that goal. This is what delivers customer satisfaction and the ultimate prize: brand loyalty.

It is, therefore, not surprising but amusing—and a sobering lesson—that the BJP's brand proposition, 'Modi Ki Guarantee', for the Lok Sabha elections 2024 barely lasted a couple of months.

Here are ten statements quoted verbatim from the BJP manifesto. The paragraphs accompanying each statement provide clues as to why the key proposition, propagated in January 2024, had virtually disappeared in the campaign by early May.

We will ensure the dignity of women:

Hathras. Unnao. Kathua. Bilkis Bano. Brij Bhushan Sharan Singh. Prajwal Revanna. Sandeskhali.

We have gone from a nation that was in the 'Fragile Five' to a nation that is one of the top five economies of the world:

Ten years ago, India was the tenth-biggest economy in the world with household financial savings at 7.2% of the GDP.[358] Today, as the fourth-largest economy, income inequality is even worse than it was during the British Raj.[359] Net financial household savings were at a fifty-year low, at 5.1% of the GDP, in 2023-24.[360]

Fifty-plus crore citizens have joined the banking system through PM Jan Dhan Account:

As of December 2023, one out of five Jan Dhan accounts created was inoperative/dormant for over two years. This translated to 10.34 crore accounts not being used at all. An amount of 12,779 crore rupees is lying unused in these dormant accounts.[361]

Four-plus crore families now have pucca houses under the PM Awas Yojana and other initiatives:

As of January 2024, one out of three houses that were sanctioned under PMAY-U were yet to be completed.[362]

Improved health care of women by making sanitary pads available at 1 rupee:

In 2019–21, one out of five women did not use hygienic methods of protection during menstruation.[363] One out of four girls either misses school during periods, or discontinues her education entirely due to inadequate facilities and other obstacles.[364]

1.4-plus crore young citizens availed skill training under the PM Kaushal Vikas Yojana:

As per the 2022-23 Standing Committee on Labour, Textiles and Skill Development, the placement rate for the PMKVY 2 stood at 23%. For PMKVY 3, it was even lower, at just 8%. As of 30 June 2022, over half of the budget allocated was unutilized.[365]

Unprecedented hike in Minimum Support Price (MSP):

Farmers protested to demand MSP as a guarantee. They were not allowed to enter Delhi, tear gassed and sprayed with water cannons. In 2024, nineteen farmers died[366] and forty got injured[367] during the Dilli Chalo protest.

Unprecedented improvements in connectivity of the Northeast by expansion of roads, bridges, railways and airports:

Out of 181 projects sanctioned under North-East Special Infrastructure Development Scheme, only twenty-five had been completed as of December 2023. In the last six years, the scheme utilized only 40% of the allocated funds.[368]

Constructed 3.7 lakh kilometre of rural roads in villages under PM Gram Sadak Yojana:

The scheme has four verticals of which none had completed all the sanctioned projects as of January 2023. Two of these verticals had a deadline of 2022. Road Connectivity Project on Left Wing Extremism Areas, which had a deadline of March 2023, only completed half of the sanctioned kilometres by then.[369]

Achieved 100% electrification by providing electricity connection to 2.8-plus crore families under Saubhagya:

According to the government's definition, a village is considered electrified if just 10% of households have electricity.[370] In 2021, as per some states, nearly 12 lakh households were yet to be electrified.[371] Moreover, according to a response by the Minister of Power in Rajya Sabha in December 2023, nearly 5 lakh households were left to be electrified in Rajasthan, Uttar Pradesh and Andhra Pradesh.[372]

'Modi ki Guarantee' was a brand proposition that the consumer did not believe. No wonder it was quickly put to bed.

14

The Twelve-Letter Word Giving the Government Sleepless Nights

The BJP floundered in the 2024 Lok Sabha election. The floundering continued on the floor of both Houses where MPs from the INDIA (Indian National Developmental Inclusive Alliance) bloc delivered multiple speeches that were well-structured, well-executed and rich in content. A recurring theme in many of these powerful interventions on the Budget 2024 was a twelve-letter word that gave Modi and his coalition sleepless Delhi nights: unemployment.

Article 41 of the Constitution states, 'The State shall, within the limits of its economic capacity and development, make effective provision for securing the right to work, to education, and to public assistance in cases of unemployment, old age, sickness and disablement, and in other cases of undeserved want.'

EMPLOYMENT AND FOOD INSECURITY

Many MPs in the Opposition quoted Centre for Monitoring Indian Economy (CMIE) data about the employment rate—which is the 'proportion of employed persons in the working age population'— recorded at 37% in June 2024.[373] The 2023 Global Hunger Index was often referred to in Parliament—India ranked 111th out of 125 countries.[374] In the 2025 Global Hunger Index, India ranked 102nd out of 123 countries Despite improvements in food production and distribution, food insecurity persists, particularly in marginalized communities.

IMPACT ON PERSONAL FREEDOMS

A citizen cannot truly enjoy any liberty when she is perpetually anxious about her family's unmet needs. This became even more important when the Union and state budgets in India skirt around the issues of health, nutrition, social security and education. It is difficult to think about personal liberties on an empty stomach.

MNREGA

MNREGA addresses the issue of Right to Work. However, it ensures it as a statutory right, instead of being a Fundamental Right. The latter cannot be taken away by an amendment of the MNREGA Act. It bears repetition that states have been constantly deprived of MNREGA funds. The Union owes the West Bengal government alone over 6,900 crore rupees vis-a-vis the scheme.[375]

In a labour-surplus society, why then was the Union government often seen selling the family silver to private entities? Two dozen large Public Sector Undertakings (PSUs) have been privatized. This was not the solution. Should it not be the duty of the State to offer the labour force multiple opportunities for employment? There were 30 lakh vacancies in the Union government and government-controlled organizations.[376] What was the road map and timelines for these vacancies to be filled? Parliament was in session. The government should have provided answers.

EDUCATION AND SKILL DEVELOPMENT

The Union has an obligation to provide quality education and skill development to improve employability and guarantee livelihood. But the revised estimates in 2024 had allocated only 1.14 lakh crore rupees to education, which was an 8% decline from Actuals (1.23 lakh crore rupees) in 2023-24.[377]

Right to Livelihood As A Fundamental Right

Through judicial interpretation, the Right to Livelihood has been read into the Right to Life, even though it is not explicitly listed among the Fundamental Rights in Part III of the Constitution. The Supreme Court emphasized, 'An equally important facet of the right to life is the right to livelihood because no person can live without the means of living, that is, the means of livelihood. If the right to livelihood is not treated as a part of the constitutional right to life, the easiest way of depriving a person of his right to life would be to deprive him of his means of livelihood to the point of abrogation. Such deprivation would not only strip life of its effective content and meaningfulness but also make life impossible to live.'

The Right to Work, outlined in the directive principles, has been interpreted alongside the Rights to Livelihood and Life, evolving into a Fundamental Right through judicial pronouncements. Integrating the Right to Work into Fundamental Rights, and ensuring that policies are designed to create sustainable job opportunities, is paramount to ensuring employment. Even after a tepid performance in the General Elections 2024, where they were punished by young people, this government refused to prioritize investment in educational and vocational training.

Additionally, fostering a more inclusive job market by supporting small businesses and encouraging entrepreneurship can play a critical role in generating employment. By taking these steps, India can align its economic policies better with its constitutional commitments and provide more meaningful support to its citizens.

The Right to Work still requires the state to take responsibility, and appropriate legislative actions, to fully provide citizens with the Right to Life, Livelihood and Dignity.

15

In Parliament, Opposition Has a New 'Josh'

'How's the josh?' was the line made famous in a not-my-kind-of-a-film which did well at the box office five years ago. Now, ask any member of the Opposition in Parliament the same question. How's the josh? There is a distinct spring in the steps of MPs from Opposition parties, both in the Lok Sabha and the Rajya Sabha.

Since the results of 2024 elections, Parliament has held six sessions. As an observer and participant, let me share five reasons which kept the Josh Quotient (JQ) of the Opposition high.

Skittish Floor Management

Compare the Budget Session of 2009, when Dr Manmohan Singh was elected for his second term, to the 2024 Budget Session where Narendra Modi (albeit with support from the National Democratic Alliance parties) began his third term.

In 2009, the House ran for thirty-three days, introducing seventeen, and passing eight, Bills. Budget Session 2024 ran for twenty-two days and then adjourned ahead of schedule. Both Houses were abruptly cut short on the afternoon of 9 August, instead of 12 August. (That the Hindenburg story broke over the intervening weekend was purely a coincidence!) There were some obvious signs of skittishness. Fourteen Bills were introduced, only three were passed. The Union government did not agree to discussions on the working of the home affairs ministry and the defence ministry, even though fifteen parties demanded that these two sensitive ministries be discussed.

LEADER OF THE OPPOSITION

For the first time in a decade, after the 2024 elections, there was a Leader of the Opposition in Lok Sabha. The Salary and Allowances of Leaders of Opposition in Parliament Act of 1977 describes the Leader of Opposition (LoP) as a member in either House who belongs to a party in Opposition with the 'greatest numerical strength'.

While the Act does not prescribe it, the convention followed (as prescribed by Lok Sabha Speaker G.V. Mavalankar in 1956) is that a party must secure at least fifty-five seats to nominate a member for the post. While the Congress had fifty-two MPs in the 17th Lok Sabha, this time with almost hundred MPs, the party officially laid claim to the position.

Constitutionally and psychologically, this really pumped up the INDIA bloc in the House of the People. Rahul Gandhi would have been happy with the runs he scored in his debut innings.

OPPOSITION FIREPOWER

Another leader, also in his fifties, with a front-row seat at the theatre of Indian democracy, is Akhilesh Yadav. The former chief minister and now MP from Kannauj is leading his team of thirty-seven MPs—up by thirty-two seats from what the Samajwadi Party (SP) had won in the 17th Lok Sabha. Also, turning on the heat is thirty-six-year-old National General Secretary of the Trinamool Congress, Abhishek Banerjee. Trinamool, too, had upped their numbers in 2024. From twenty-two to twenty-nine, including eleven female MPs.

Rahul Gandhi's maiden speech as Leader of Opposition, with the theme of Shiva and non-violence, most certainly got under the skin of the BJP. Akhilesh Yadav was in his element too, slamming the government on examination paper leaks. Speaking on the Budget, Banerjee's forty-five-minute speech and interaction with the Lok Sabha Speaker went viral for all the right reasons. Here was a three-time MP showing the Chair utmost respect and yet firmly making his point—why the objection to him speaking about demonetization that happened eight years ago, when BJP MPs were allowed to talk about Pandit Nehru and the Emergency from decades ago?

Gandhi, Yadav and Banerjee, charged with 164 MPs between the trio, are a potent force on the floor of Lok Sabha. The three have contrasting styles of delivery, but are high on content and political nuance.

A strong contingent of MPs from Tamil Nadu, Kerala and members of the Maharashtra Vikas Aghadi also weighed in on issues of national importance.

From Bengal to Tamil Nadu, from Uttar Pradesh to Maharashtra, the Opposition was backed by the assuredness and guidance of popular or former Chief Ministers, and by a genuine appeal among citizens tired of local BJP/NDA governments in the aftermath of the 2024 elections.

The Opposition represented the pulse, energy and diversity of India. The government stood for jaded Delhi power brokers and neo-elites of Lutyens'.

BJP's New Parliamentary Team

Even though Narendra Modi decided to brave it out and not change portfolios of ministers handling key ministries, the ruling dispensation did opt for a comparatively new team to run Parliament. J.P. Nadda was appointed Leader of the House in Rajya Sabha, replacing Piyush Goyal who won his Lok Sabha seat. The seemingly more affable Kiren Rijiju replaced Pralhad Joshi as Minister of Parliamentary Affairs. First-time MP L. Murugan, from Tamil Nadu, was made the new Minister of State (MoS) for Parliamentary Affairs.

THE SONIA GANDHI EFFECT

In 2024, the five-term Lok Sabha MP was also making her debut in the Council of States. She chose not to make her maiden speech in Rajya Sabha or to intervene in the twenty-two days when Parliament was in session. Even without switching the microphone on, her actions, demeanour and gestures invigorated the twenty-six Congress MPs. Her presence also had a great unifying effect on the INDIA bloc. Josh!

16

Here's an Unlikely Combination: Narendra Modi and Billy Joel

In his last two terms as Prime Minister, between 2014 and 2024, Mr Modi has done all it takes to turn Parliament into a deep, dark chamber, as previously argued. Early in 2024, after a long gap of thirty years, one of my favourite singer-songwriters, the legendary Billy Joel, released a new song titled 'Turn the Lights Back On'.

That was the verdict after the 2024 General Elections, it seems. The Lok Sabha and the Rajya Sabha cannot be allowed to be turned into a deep, dark chamber. Turn on the lights back on, the voter has demanded.

Let's get this done. Here are some of my suggestions to make it happen:

Parliament Calendar

As I have already mentioned in the book, we need to introduce a fixed calendar for the three sessions of Parliament with a minimum of 100 days of sittings a year for each House. The number of sittings per year for Lok Sabha has reduced from an average of 121 days (1952–1970) to seventy days per year since 2000.[378] As you would recall, in 2019, I introduced a Private Member's Bill seeking a fixed calendar for Parliament sessions and a minimum number of sittings of 100 days. The

17th Lok Sabha held a total of 274 sittings, with only four previous Lok Sabhas having fewer, all of which were dissolved before completing their five-year terms. Remarkably, eleven out of the fifteen sessions during this Lok Sabha were adjourned ahead of schedule.[379]

DEPUTY SPEAKER IN LOK SABHA

Article 93 of the Constitution says that the Lok Sabha shall choose two members of the House as Speaker and Deputy Speaker as soon as the case may be. The 17th Lok Sabha did not have a Deputy Speaker for its entire five-year term. The Deputy Speaker is not subordinate to the Speaker. The Speaker has to tender his resignation to the Deputy Speaker, if they choose to do so. Traditionally, the Deputy Speaker is appointed from the Opposition. The Deputy Speaker has still not been appointed. The post remains unfilled since June 2023.

PRE-LEGISLATIVE CONSULTATION POLICY

Pre-Legislative Consultation Policy was adopted in 2014 to ensure public consultation for all legislation. In the 17th Lok Sabha, nine out of ten bills introduced in Parliament were marked by zero or incomplete consultations. Each minister, while introducing a Bill, should lay a copy of the summary of the consultations.

SCRUTINY OF BILLS

In the 14th Lok Sabha, six out of ten bills were sent to various committees for scrutiny; in the 15th Lok Sabha, it was seven out of ten. This figure fell in the 16th Lok Sabha to four out of ten. In the 17th Lok Sabha, about one out of five Bills was sent for scrutiny. Abysmal. The National Commission to Review the Working of the Constitution (2002) recommended that all Bills introduced in Parliament should first be examined by the relevant committee.[380] Committees should also review the implementation of laws passed by Parliament.

Constitution Amendment Bills

A joint constitutional committee from both Houses should be formed to review the constitutional validity of Constitution Amendment Bills before they are introduced.

Admit 267 Notice in Rajya Sabha

Rule 267 gives Rajya Sabha MPs an opportunity to give a written notice to suspend regular business and seek an immediate discussion on an issue of national importance. It has been nearly ten years since such a discussion has been permitted. At least one such notice should be admitted in each session.

Active Participation of PM

The Prime Minister has not answered a single question on the floor of Parliament during his tenure. His participation has been limited to monologues—speeches during the Motion of Thanks, farewells and special occasions. Narendra Modi needs to answer questions, take part in debates and discussions on national issues. (The United Kingdom Parliament has Prime Minister's Question Time every Wednesday, where it is mandatory for the PM to respond.)

Joint Parliamentary Committee on Security

Following the Parliament security breach in 2023, the committee on security in Parliament house complex should have been reconstituted immediately, with the Deputy Speaker as the Chairperson. We need better systems in place to not only curtail such cowardly attacks but also address, investigate and resolve them.

Committee on National Economy

A Parliamentary Committee on National Economy should be formed to produce annual reports on the state of the economy. The report should then be discussed in Parliament. The National Commission to Review the Working of the Constitution (2002) noted that there is no system for parliamentary scrutiny of public borrowing. Since it affects future governments, beyond certain limits, borrowing proposals should also be reviewed by the Parliamentary Committee on National Economy.

Technical Expertise for Committees

Funds should be allocated to provide research support staff to committees, to conduct public hearings, inquiries and collect data. Currently, the secretariat assists with scheduling meetings and taking notes. The quality of output will improve if each committee is assigned a team dedicated to research.

~

Please open the door
Nothing is different, we've been here before
Pacing these halls
Trying to talk over the silence
And pride sticks out its tongue
Laughs at the portrait that we've become
Stuck in a frame, unable to change
I was wrong
Did I wait too long
To turn the lights back on?

—Billy Joel, 'Turn the Lights Back On'

17

New Parliament Should Get Rid of Bad Laws

Narendra Modi's BJP won the popular mandate and ran the government in India for ten years. In the summer of 2024, that BJP government was down to a number below the majority mark of 272 seats in Lok Sabha. So, we had a new starting point for the 18th Lok Sabha. A coalition government. Which perhaps could mean better accountability at the legislative level. To ensure justice, equality and liberty for all citizens, the following laws should be reconsidered and repealed by this government.

CITIZENSHIP AMENDMENT ACT

As the Citizenship Amendment Bill was introduced in Parliament in 2019, the country protested over concerns that, coupled with the proposed National Register of Citizens (NRC), could lead to the disenfranchisement of many Indian citizens. Home Minister Amit Shah insisted that the NRC would be implemented nationwide, despite the disastrous pilot project in Assam—where around 6% of residents were left out of the final NRC list. If this exclusion rate is extrapolated nationally, crores of Indians could potentially become stateless.

Criminal Law Bills

The recent, arbitrarily enacted Criminal Law bills require urgent reconsideration and should be repealed, since they gloss over the provisions on marital rape and sedition, and pose the risk of 'police raj' by criminalizing 'resisting, refusing, ignoring or disregarding to conform to any direction given by a police officer'. This is a slippery slope to authoritarianism and undermines fundamental freedoms. The devil is in the details. These laws, with their significant discrepancies and inherent injustices, need thorough scrutiny and stakeholder consultations. (I was a member of the Parliamentary Standing Committee on Home Affairs where constructive suggestions and voices of dissent from members of the Opposition were ignored in the final recommendations.)

Marital Rape Exception

Section 63 of the Bharatiya Nyaya Sanhita deals with the offence of rape, but provides an exception for marital rape, stating that 'sexual intercourse or sexual acts by a man with his own wife, the wife not being under eighteen years of age, is not rape'. This exception stems from archaic English laws that did not recognize men and women as equals. It undermines the fundamental principle that rape is a violation of personal autonomy and bodily integrity, regardless of the relationship between the perpetrator and the victim. It's high time we bid farewell to this outdated notion.

Sedition

The use of Section 124A of the Indian Penal Code (the old sedition law) had been kept in abeyance following a Supreme Court order in May 2022. The court had given the government time to reconsider the law. Subsequently, the Home Minister claimed that sedition has been removed from the list of offences in the Bharatiya Nyaya Sanhita.

This new version avoids the term 'sedition', but introduces a vaguely defined offence of 'endangering the sovereignty, unity, and integrity of India'. This broad definition, contrary to the 22nd Law Commission's recommendation for clarity, leaves room for misuse, and threatens to stifle dissent and protest.

The Chief Election Commissioner and other Election Commissioners Act, 2023

The Act changes the composition of the selection committee to appoint Election Commissioners. The Supreme Court's directive that the Chief Justice should be a part of the committee was disregarded. The Prime Minister, Leader of the Opposition and a nominated Union cabinet minister now make the selection, giving the Union government disproportionate control over the selection.

The Mines and Minerals (Development and Regulation) Amendment Act, 2023

The Act empowered the Union government to exclusively auction mining leases and composite exploration licences for certain critical high-value minerals, such as cadmium, selenium, nickel, cobalt, tin, etc. It also dispensed with the forest clearances required for mine reconnaissance and prospecting operations. It is critical to point out that the Act allows sub-surface excavation as part of reconnaissance, which had been prohibited under the original 1957 Act. The environmental consequences of such invasive operations can be severe and irreversible, undermining sustainable development goals and disregarding previously existing environmental protections.

The Transgender Persons Act, 2019

The Transgender Persons (Protection of Rights) Act, 2019, only recognizes 'sexual abuse' with a maximum punishment of two years as opposed to life imprisonment for rape of women. This punishment is insufficient and discriminatory. The law on rape should be inclusive and extend its protection to transgender women, ensuring they receive the same legal safeguards and justice as cisgender women.

18

Twelve New MPs to Watch Out For

Of the 543 MPs in the 18th Lok Sabha, 280 are spanking new—in their first few months of service at the time of writing. Add to that the 166 MPs who have been in Rajya Sabha for around a year. That's 446 MPs (of the total 770 MPs) who could be informally described as 'newbies' in Parliament. Wish I could write a paragraph about each new parliamentarian. Since that cannot happen, let me introduce you to twelve new Opposition MPs to watch out for.

LOK SABHA

Alfred Kan-Ngam Arthur, Indian National Congress, Manipur

'If the Prime Minister cannot bring peace in a small state like mine, what will he manage in such a big country as ours?'

Sharp. Direct. Addressing the Speaker with the swagger of a veteran. Mr Kan-Ngam Arthur is unplugged, unedited. He is one of the two Lok Sabha representatives from Manipur. He made a mark in his first speech in Parliament, clearly articulating how he, as a member of the Naga community—the only neutral party in the conflict—must be utilized to instil and restore peace in Manipur.

SAAYONI GHOSH, ALL INDIA TRINAMOOL CONGRESS, WEST BENGAL

'Through their mandate for me, the people of Jadavpur have sent the message that Bengal has no place for the politics of hatred and manipulation.'

Former actor. President of the youth wing of her party. She won from Jadavpur, the same seat won by her leader Mamata Banerjee forty years ago. She is in the contingent of eleven female MPs from the Trinamool Congress in Lok Sabha. In her maiden speech, Ms Ghosh had the visible self-assuredness of a remarkably talented trilingual communicator.

IQRA CHOUDHARY, SAMAJWADI PARTY, UTTAR PRADESH

'As a member who has till recently been a student, I would like to shed light on facets that aren't as rosy as the government might think.'

Before she could be (predictably) patronized for her youth, Ms Choudhary, speaking on the Demands for Grants for the Ministry of Education, underlined the need to institutionally empower women in heavily patriarchal constituencies like the one she represents. Fascinating.

CAPTAIN VIRIATO FERNANDES, INDIAN NATIONAL CONGRESS, GOA

'The Railways is trying to increase its revenue through freight. The most important cargo they are targeting is coal. In 2018, Prime Minister Modi was conferred the title "Champion of Earth". Ironically, coal is detrimental to the environment. We are speaking opposite languages.'

Twenty-six years in the Indian Navy. Operation Vijay Star and Operation Vijay Medal awardee for service in the Kargil War of 1999. His gentle manners, unassuming demeanour and sharp communication skills will work wonders in the Lok Sabha. South Goa was a copybook seat for the INDIA bloc and much of that credit goes to this comparatively new Congressman who knows how to win friends and influence people.

Chandrashekhar Azad, Aazad Samaj Party (Kanshi Ram) Uttar Pradesh

'The country is as much theirs as ours. We weren't born to die.'

A few political pundits believe he might turn out to be the post-Bahujan Samaj Party Dalit leader—a space that Mayawati has given up. For now, his victory from Nagina has solidified Mr Azad's evolution from activist to a people's leader. As the only member from his party, built on one laser-focused argument: the Constitution is my only calling card. The blue scarf around his neck is a simple, powerful visual mnemonic that's here to stay.

Priya Saroj, Samajwadi Party, Uttar Pradesh

'The BJP says sabka saath, sabka vikas. *But they've only done their own* vikas. *India's citizens have woken up.'*

Another infusion of young blood by Team Akhilesh Yadav. Ms Saroj's maiden speech was on the Demands for Grants for the Ministry of Education. She seemed unfazed by the monstrosity of the moment. She represents a crucial, almost unchartered intersection, even within the Samajwadi Party—a young Dalit woman enthusiastic to navigate the road of public service.

Aga Syed Ruhullah Mehdi, Jammu & Kashmir National Conference, Jammu & Kashmir

'Members of this House are lucky to have normal circumstances. That they are equal citizens of this country. That they can participate in this debate. We do not have this luxury ... We are not servants of your will.'

This speech of his coincided with the fifth anniversary of the abrogation of Article 370. Mr Mehdi was often shouted down by the Treasury Benches and 'censored'. Tackling all these with consummate ease, his rejoinder: have the spine to listen.

Dr Prabha Mallikarjun, Indian National Congress, Karnataka

'If only the Centre knew one or two billionaires to help them out! Start alphabetically with "A" and they might find someone.'

Born into an agriculturalist family, the debutant MP is a dentist by training. The charming Dr Mallikarjun is one of about thirty MPs belonging to the medical fraternity. Her intervention in the Demands for Grants for the Ministry of Health and Family Welfare had six sharp pointers on how health is underfunded and overlooked by the government. She argued that the Union budget only had incremental changes and not the vision needed to transform the sector.

Awadhesh Prasad, Samajwadi Party, Uttar Pradesh

'I went through the seventy-page Budget document not once but several times. Even with binoculars, there is no mention of Ayodhya or Uttar Pradesh. In the name of Ayodhya, the BJP has only carried out politics and business, and completely ignored its development.'

Nine-time MLA. Former minister in the state government. He was tipped to be INDIA bloc's chosen candidate for the post of Deputy Speaker in Lok Sabha. In more ways than one, Awadhesh Prasad is the man of the hour. He defeated the BJP where it hurt the most—Ayodhya. In his response to the Budget, Mr Prasad called the government out for exploiting his constituency for political advantage. His message was simple: people's houses were bulldozed and their businesses were stopped; they are not going to forgive the BJP.

RAJYA SABHA

HARIS BEERAN, INDIAN UNION MUSLIM LEAGUE, KERALA

'The President is an icon of women's empowerment and determination. It is sad to see that the Government has forced her to read a script which is far from the truth.'

The Supreme Court lawyer from Kerala is the newest addition to the INDIA contingent in Rajya Sabha. Mr Beeran debuted by playing to his strengths. Clearly articulated views on the caste census, the new criminal laws and the enfranchisement rights for migrant workers. Sparkling start.

SANJAY YADAV, RASHTRIYA JANATA DAL, BIHAR

'This Budget is not for our sons. It is for the sons of the rich. This Budget is not for the weak and poor. It is for the strong and powerful. This Budget is not for the development of the marginalized. It is to ridicule them.'

Tejaswi Yadav's trusted aide will certainly make his mark in the Council of States. Young, down to earth, well-educated with a deep understanding of his state, Bihar, he is bound to sparkle.

SAKET GOKHALE, ALL INDIA TRINAMOOL CONGRESS, WEST BENGAL

'The Union Budget by the finance minister reminds me of an old quote by Benjamin Franklin: "Nothing is certain except death and taxes." The finance minister's taxes are worse. Death kills you only once in your life, these taxes kill you every year.'

Once a war correspondent, then a Right to Information activist and now one of the youngest members in Rajya Sabha, Mr Gokhale represents West Bengal. (I am leaving out the 150-day political imprisonment for speaking up against the government).

While speaking on the Union budget for 2024-25, he highlighted the government's systematic deprivation of opposition states like West Bengal, a tax regime that is disproportionately skewed against the middle and lower classes, and their brazen mistreatment of minorities.

19

POLLS AND PREDICTIONS

There are a few times in a year, when everyone—from your neighbour to your niece in her second year of undergraduate studies—turns into a pundit, psephologist and analyst. Tempers sizzle. Passions and decibel levels rise. TV screens are inundated with grids of neon, flashing large digits and sensational tickers. Large panels congregate. Squabbles break out on live TV. News anchors are heard shouting across living rooms as India 'tunes in', half-disagreeing, half-checked out, folding the day's laundry and thinking about what to eat for lunch tomorrow. But still able to disassociate from the carnival on their screens.

For some, the cynicism has crept in. Think of your uncle with his paunch, one hand resting on his hip as he declares, 'How does it matter?' For others, indifference may have become a coping mechanism. Your younger brother who passes by, witnessing the madness on TV, muttering with disdain, 'All fudged data'. Or on the opposite end, your mother, eyes tracking every digit change as she narrates how in 1998, the forecasting was accurate—she is still hopeful.

At this stage, my dear reader, I must make clear the forecasting I am referring to. If at the time of reading this book, you are twenty-two and above, some of these descriptions may bring back some memories. If you're around thirty-five, you know exactly what I am talking about.

And if you're older still, you detest that you know exactly what I am talking about. Yes, predictions for electoral polls.

Predicting election results is not a new phenomenon. However, in recent years, the reliability of these predictions has become suspicious. Consider this: It is widely acknowledged that the first ever exit poll in India was conducted in 1957 by an organization called the Indian Institute of Public Opinion, headed by Eric De Costa. De Costa, often called India's 'first pollster', applied statistical tools to measure what he called the 'index of Opposition unity'. To this day, no archival records of this have been found. Perhaps it was a quiet academic exercise.

Cut to the 2020s.

We see these images often enough on polling days and then election result days: video journalists thrusting out their boom microphones. Reporters brushing past one another to deliver the most arresting but short-lived sound byte. We live in the age of half-baked questions on the move. Answers that lose their relevance and impact within a few hours. In the last decade or so, those making poll predictions in India have also lost some credibility. Even though factors like staggered polling schedules and seat sharing under the first-past-the-post system may pose some challenges, the harshest critics of these forecasters now ask, are they really forecasting or has this become a game of 'pinning the tail on the donkey'?

Have polling agencies, who send out hard-working field surveyors, armed with smartphones, forgotten who the Indian voter really is? That citizens live in areas beyond WiFi coverage and concrete highways? In the last decade alone, there has been a predictable exclusion in whom pollsters choose to speak with. Election after election, voters covered in surveys do not capture the diversity of the demographic. This means, after the data is collected, algorithms have to be deployed to simulate 'normalized vote share'. This bias in data collection—typically, an over-representation of urban, male, educated voters, and an under-representation of rural, lower-income respondents—leads to erroneous predictions. Let us look at three examples.

After the Lok Sabha elections of 2014, one widely followed exit poll was as many as sixty-six seats off the mark while predicting NDA's seat share. This anomaly was later attributed to an insufficient coverage of first-time and rural voters. In the 2016 West Bengal assembly elections, exit polls predicted All India Trinamool Congress (AITC) to win around 175 seats. The actual result? AITC won 211 seats. The error of thirty-six seats was due to undersampling of rural and low-income groups. In 2024, forecasting the NDA's seat share was way off the mark again. This time by over seventy-seven seats. The error? Over-representation of urban voters in the sample. Bias is prevalent not simply in what sample sizes are chosen but also in the 'turn-out models' used to forecast. Simply put, turn-out models use past election data and demographic assumptions to make predictions. It is similar to how you predict who will show up to your birthday party from the group of friends you invite each year. You look at who has shown up in the past and how frequently, who always claims they 'will 100% be there' but never are, those perpetually in the 'dicey' category and those who leave your WhatsApp message unread. In the same way, turnout patterns in Indian elections have undergone significant transformation. The statistical models being used have not factored in these recent trends. Professor Sanjay Kumar, an election analyst, explained to me, 'Many exit polls are missing out on proper methodology of sampling, using the convenience method of sampling. Some polls are also using shortcuts in field work, winding up the data collection much before the voting ends. This is being done to catch up to the TV programme deadline of 6 p.m.' He also said, 'We should not forget, social media is also having an effect on vote choice, which some of the analysis fails to take into account and far more importance is still being placed on caste community-based voting analysis.' V.K. Bajaj, co-founder of Today's Chanakya, seemed to echo Kumar's line of thought: 'Polls done can give a correct idea of the likely outcome, provided these polls are executed scientifically. It is quite possible to get an accurate assessment if the right sampling methodology is followed and the sample drawn is truly representative, reflecting ground realities. We do not need a big sample size but we need a representative sample.' An example of this could be seen in the Lok Sabha elections of 2019. For the first time in electoral history, the national turnout of women voters (67.18%) exceeded the male turnout (67.01%). Pollsters who continued to interview less women in their sample survey ended up with flawed predictions.

What the Indian election prediction business seems to have forgotten is that predicting results is not just driven by pie charts and bar graphs. Pollsters today would benefit by readjusting their perspective to place *people* at the centre of their analysis. Founder and director of Axis My India, Pradeep Gupta explained to me: 'Axis My India has accurately predicted seventy-six of eighty-one elections, often with sample sizes below 0.1%. While minor deviations can occur, the real value of exit polls lies beyond forecasting results—by helping understand voting behaviour, key issues, citizen expectation, and providing a practical lens into public sentiments and priorities. This is relevant for governance and policy responses.' Here's an example of how the opposite happens. Often amongst highly polarized or socially stratified groups, respondents tend to withhold their true political preferences when asked about it point-blank. The risk involved in answering a stranger's question is too high: backlash from the immediate environment they exist in, for one. Behavioural psychology 101. Surya A.V., a seasoned research professional, shared the technical term for this with me: 'social desirability bias'. It seems, however, that most polling 'experts' are blind to this well-known phenomenon. In 2014, for example, surveys massively underestimated BJP support in states such as Uttar Pradesh and Bihar by 5–7 percentage points because respondents in 'regional-party-dominated areas' were reluctant to disclose their preferences. In Tamil Nadu and Bihar, respondents have been found to give 'courtesy responses', naming locally dominant parties rather than their actual choice. Should their inhibition not be factored in? In Bengal, a similar oversight occurred in 2021. Sections of Muslims and female voters (rightfully) viewed pollsters as outsiders, and were hesitant to reveal their preference to them. No poll considered this in their margin of error. Almost all of them made bold declarations of a 'narrow contest'. The actual results were often the exact opposite.

In 2024, as a widely watched TV channel discussed (read: tried to make sense of) the embarrassingly wide gap between the actual results and predictions they had made, a moment of reckoning took place. The haughty anchor, one of the many BJP pin-up boys, stood next to a bright red screen flashing the results. He made a feeble attempt to mask his disbelief with a diffident, 'There seems to be a variation in the vote share the post-poll studies came back with and the actual vote share.' In the same multi-cam studio, a high-profile psephologist broke down in tears. Failure went viral. The anchor, quick to cover up, continued: '[Exit] polls are always directional. They are never the gospel truth.' A casual brush off. Should newsrooms of one of the most esteemed channels in India not take ownership for kite-flying exit polls? If you want to take all the credit when you get it right, then you also have to put your hand up when you fail miserably. The convergence of polling and broadcast media has created an environment where agencies often align their forecasts within a set range to avoid being seen as outliers. To put it in simpler terms, imagine you and your group of friends are predicting who will win the FIFA World Cup this year. Maybe three of them say Brazil, and four say Argentina. You might think Croatia has a good chance, but the fear of being an outlier might lead you to choose either Brazil or Argentina. The same principle applies here. Herd mentality reinforces systematic bias: multiple agencies err in the same direction, producing the illusion of accuracy through consensus. In 2024, nine major national polls projected NDA seat counts between 353 and 401. The actual figure was 293. A similar trend was evident in West Bengal in 2021. Virtually every exit poll predicted a close contest. No agency reported a landslide projection for AITC, even though internal constituency-level data later revealed strong margins.

Let's give the last word to the GOAT of election analysis in India, Dr Prannoy Roy. Here is what he told me: 'The rapid growth in opinion polls and exit polls over the years in India is something to be proud of. The accuracy of opinion polls is 75%. While this is still a little below global standards, our fragmented political system with multiple parties makes polling more complex. There is little doubt, though, that what is needed is more transparency and rigour. We need to create a set of rules ourselves—do not leave rule creation to the government. Rules which ensure that only polls that meet these criteria are published. Most importantly, polling agencies need to include 50% women interviewers. Women in our villages respond more openly to female interviewers.'

In 1994, American scientist George Loewenstein came up with the 'Information Gap Theory'. Loewenstein asked participants obscure trivia questions and asked them to rate their curiosity. As they did this, he scanned their brains to understand neural reactions. Loewenstein's study revealed a simple truth: curiosity arises when a person becomes aware of a gap between what they know and what they want (or need) to know. According to Loewenstein, this gap is not just neutral: it produces a mental state of *deprivation,* which motivates a person to seek out the missing information. In the past decade, exit polls in India zeroed in on this gap in our psyche, and made it their mission to change it to a (perpetual) state of deprivation. Every miss and mistake widened the gap between what we know and what we wanted to know. Repeated over time, this became a means to keep the state of deprivation alive. And somewhere between the blitzy screens and self-validating 'expert panels', exploitation of curiosity became a revenue model.

MEDIA

1

It is Time for Politician–Journalists

What exactly is happening (or more correctly, not happening) at the altar of democracy—Parliament?

Scenes that one views on Sansad TV are being selectively edited online before telecast. Protests by Opposition MPs are rarely, if ever, shown. The edited video output ensures the focus is on the Speaker, Chairperson and the Treasury Benches. Visuals of Opposition MPs protesting from their seats or in the well of the House are censored.[381] Sansad TV is not the only culprit. Media outlets too have their own priorities.

There is no use being a crybaby. No use sitting around complaining about pro-establishment reportage. Political parties in the Opposition will have to overcome these challenges through innovative ways. I feel, besides professional journalists and citizen journalists, the time is now ripe for 'politician–journalists', who must set the narrative in a proactive manner by creating compelling communication (even if it means shooting on personal mobile phones) and then amplifying the same beyond the legacy media.

The eight years I spent in my twenties in the creative department of that brilliant advertising agency, Ogilvy & Mather, come in handy today. Generating political content that cuts through the clutter is a challenge. We are moving into an era where political parties fighting the good fight will not wait for a guest relation executive from Noida to call a spokesperson to appear on prime time television. Where choreographed conclaves and soporific summits will be called out as advertorials for the ruling party. Where those taking on the Union government will create more ingenious media spaces to directly engage with the citizen.

Serious issues about Parliament are not getting many centimetres of coverage in newspapers and are most often ignored by news channels. I do believe it's the MPs from the Opposition parties who are being compelled to play the role of content creators and amplifiers as 'politician journalists'.

Scribes covering Parliament are slowly being made to play diminishing roles by a government that wants total control. Senior editors, who until not so long ago had access to Central Hall, are now not allowed into this sanctum sanctorum. No political party has conducted a formal press conference in Parliament House in at least a few years. Entry of journalists has also been restricted; lots are drawn and those whose names come up are given entry passes.

2

The Disinformation Playbook: A Government that Wants to Fact-Check the Fact-Checkers

The media is supposed to fact-check the government. Now, the government has the power to fact-check the fact-checkers. How much more brazen can we get?

Exhibit A:

Amit Shah, 2018 rally in Rajasthan (translated): 'We are capable of delivering any message we want to the public, whether sweet or sour, true or fake. We can do this work only because we have 32 lakh people in our WhatsApp groups.'[382]

Exhibit B:

J.P. Nadda, 2023 rally in Karnataka: 'No other Prime Minister in the history of India has been as great as Modi ji. He stopped the Russia–Ukraine War to evacuate 22,500 students from there back to India.'[383] This claim, made earlier by others too, had already been debunked, not by any foreign agency but India's spokesperson from the Ministry of External Affairs.

The Union government has appointed itself as a fact-checking unit![384] In what seems to be a glaring oversight, it has failed to define the fundamentals such as 'fake', 'false' and 'misleading'.

Fact-checking as a Business

With around 500 million (50 crore) WhatsApp users, and 300 million (30 crore) Facebook users, India can claim to be the world's largest fact-checking space. As of mid-2024, seventeen organizations are certified by the International Fact-Checking Network (IFCN) in India. These include standalone fact-checking platforms and multiple news organizations that have in-house fact-checking platforms. In the absence of a defined standard operating procedure, IFCN has become the single point of authority. Also, all funds are funnelled through them. This often means they unilaterally decide who gets to be a verified fact-checker.

To an extent, fact-checking has now become a business. An organization does X number of fact-checks and gets paid, corresponding to the number of fact-checks that they do. It's about the quantity—there's no one to check the quality. In this environment, even the most trivial claims are fact-checked to meet monthly billing targets.

Youth in metro cities spend more than three hours every day accessing content on their mobile phones. Extrapolate this number across a country with a population of 1.4 billion. Where will this content come from? Content creators have realized that the more provocative the content (irrespective of facts) the more views they get, and the more money they will make. While this technically invites more fact-checkers to the space, in the absence of a defined standard for the quality of fact-checking, the output suffers.

The Role of Big Tech

Equally damning are the standby companies like Meta (formerly named Facebook, Inc.) refusing to fact-check politicians. Founder Mark Zuckerberg has gone on record multiple times to state Facebook's unwillingness to fact-check politicians as they are already 'over scrutinized'. Sitting in San Francisco, their myopic views are far removed from the sociopolitical dynamics of countries like India.

Since Facebook, as a policy, does not fact-check politicians, fact-checking partners do not see any utility in doing the same. The reason is simple: no one is going to pay for these fact-checks. It is common knowledge that Facebook's fact-checking partners don't often fact-check content created by the BJP. Repeat offenders like the BJP's IT cell and its troll army have earned themselves quite a reputation.

If the government truly wanted to solve this (mis)information crisis, it might have been a good idea to look for benchmarks. Alt News, a website established in 2017, has swiftly set standards in fact-checking.

In the fight against disinformation, the root cause of the problem is the lack of credible media content and literacy. Producing fact-checks is a significant but short-term solution. The challenge is to make general users acquire the basic skills to identify malicious information and curb its dissemination.

Nexus to Create Narratives

There have been multiple instances where innocent people have been targeted on the basis of outlandish rumours spread on social media; from being suspected as child kidnappers and being blamed for spreading Covid, to accusations of eating beef, Muslims in India are at the receiving end of fake news narratives every single day. Spreading disinformation to gain political mileage is a classic move from the BJP playbook. I spoke to Alt News co-founder Pratik Sinha who was convinced that 'narratives are formed through a nexus between mainstream and social media. Such narratives often lead to economic exclusion, unlawful arrest, and hate crimes'.

Just busting fake news isn't enough. It is time to take this war on disinformation to another level. Who better to start with than school students? Realizing such an initiative would be smothered in Gujarat, Alt News shifted its base from Ahmedabad to Kolkata to upskill school students at a systemic level. In the long term, the only way to navigate this powerful and toxic ecosystem is to raise awareness among our youth.

3

How Digital Platforms Overtook Traditional Media to Reach the Voters in 2024

Six weeks, thousands of registered political parties, 97 crore eligible voters.[385] India's General Elections of 2024 were the biggest in history. Also a feasting ground for a post-truth, post-climate change democracy. With summertime temperatures climbing up to forty-five degrees and higher in various parts of the country, campaigning and running the election machine was extremely challenging for political parties. A stifling media environment with legacy news channels and most leading newspapers held captive by the ruling establishment and Prime Minister Narendra Modi's government added to the uphill task for all Opposition parties.

We, in the Opposition—struggling to breathe in the limited space India's Modi-fied democracy allowed us—were not the only ones trying to cope. The hapless Indian voter was also desperately attempting to keep herself informed and aware as she determined her franchise. What were the issues and themes that resonated with her or her fellow citizens? What was the truth behind the battery of data and the information blitz coming her way from the BJP and the government? In a media environment of compromise and negotiable facts, how does one delineate right from wrong? Simply put, how do you get the other point of view?

There was a time when this was easy and simple in India. That was also an easier and simpler India. There were honest, no-holds-barred debates and discussions on news television. Newspaper reports were trusted—they were bipartisan, if not neutral; speeches and manifestos of all major political parties were laid out threadbare. Today, India has 5,500 daily newspapers[386] and 388 news channels,[387] and yet the previously independent voice of media speaks in hushed tones. Encouraged by craven media barons, virtually every network and most publications have turned into unabashed cheerleaders of the status quo.

What is this doing to political communication in what is still the world's largest democracy? It's putting power in the voter's hands, literally! The mobile phone has become the most potent election weapon—the ultimate medium of outreach and empowerment. That India has the biggest national YouTube audience—over 46 crore people[388]—is, in a sense, an indictment of the country's formal or 'legacy media' landscape and its fading credibility. Digital media and independent platforms rewrote the rules of political communication during the last elections. To take one example, Ravish Kumar, a prominent and gutsy newscaster, was edged out of the NDTV network after it was bought over by a pro-BJP business tycoon. Today, Kumar runs his own YouTube channel. It has over 1.4 crore subscribers.

There are many other former and formal journalists who have followed that route. Perhaps even more exciting—or sobering, for old-style media—is the new breed of citizen journalists. Very often, Dhruv Rathee gets lakhs of views in the span of four to five hours after posting a video; his YouTube feed has over 3 crore subscribers. He's no trained journalist—just an engineer with a nose for research, a flair for prose and a hard-hitting style that conquers even his home-made video skills.

Prime Minister Modi himself is not unknown to this format. With over 3 crore subscribers on YouTube, he's the most followed politician on the platform. But unlike television and nine out of ten newspapers, where friends and officials can 'manage' the competition, digital media isn't an opinion monopoly in India. Not yet. The past year has seen the emergence of the 'politician–journalist'; largely, MPs from the Opposition who have devised a new strategy to challenge legacy media. Rather than send articles that are rarely printed on editorial pages and give interviews that are cut to caricatures—or appear on channels where they would be shouted down and crowded out by biased anchors and other establishment proxies—they have set up their own platforms for direct digital outreach.

The tech is rudimentary—it could even mean shooting or recording videos on mobile phones. But the uptake has been fascinating. The disintermediation of political communication, reaching voters directly and bypassing distrusted go-betweens, is exciting. It revolutionized election communication, with virtual engagement taking the place of large public meetings that are not always feasible in the summer heat. Kapil Sibal, an erudite lawyer–Parliamentarian and former minister, launched his own YouTube channel too. He says he intends to encourage an easy conversation that brings him to the 'doorsteps of Indian citizens'.

This was the big story of the 2024 elections: a digital insurgency that upturned the mechanics of political communication. Maybe it's also the future of politics in our unequal world.

4

How to be a Visible Politician

When Donald Trump took the stage at the Capital One Arena in Washington, DC for a post-inaugural rally in 2025, he had an unlikely hero to thank for his victory. Not a Silicon Valley technocrat. Not a trusted DC campaign manager. Not a donor. Instead, a first-year student at New York University.

Correction: his son, a first- year student at New York University.

As the eighteen-year old Barron Trump rose from his seat and waved with aplomb, the 47th President of the United States explained: it was Barron's idea for him to be interviewed on independent platforms. Rough estimates suggest Trump appeared on at least fourteen podcasts and interviews.[389] He chatted about the existence of Martians on one, sports on another and election fraud on most. Comedians, former footballers, scientists and ex-drug addicts—everyone interviewed Trump. Mass appeal was the only criteria. Apparently, Barron's strategy worked. His father said during his speech that he had secured the youth vote by thirty-six points.

Is there a lesson here for politicians in India?

Around the same time as the US elections, we discussed the President's Address in Parliament. Many members of the Opposition from both Houses made compelling arguments. To expose the policies of the Union government, I invoked ten iconic films that were India's

221

official entries to the Oscars. One mainline English daily and all Bengali newspapers reported the speech. That's it. Not a line in any other newspaper. Not five seconds on television. What, then, does a politician from the Opposition do? First, stop complaining. Then, look for solutions instead.

As this writer has said before, this is the time for the politician–journalist. The first move after a speech is delivered in Parliament (and broadcast live by Sansad TV) is to upload the video on all personal social media platforms and also share it in multiple WhatsApp groups. What happened with my speech on the President's Address was a pleasant surprise! A Malayalam YouTube channel picked up the speech and uploaded it: over 48,000 views drawn promptly (and counting).[390] A Bengali YouTube channel shared the speech: over 40,000 views and counting.[391] An independent English video platform next: over 30,000 views and counting.[392]

We could broadly classify the consumption of political news content under three different kinds of media platforms:

LEGACY MEDIA

This includes newspapers and television channels. Also referred to as 'mainstream media'; the phrase 'legacy media' seems more appropriate. International trends suggest that this segment still occupies mindspace in influencing opinion. Here too, the worst affected is what is known as 'appointment television'—a phrase that derives from watching a specific programme on television at an appointed time. Is television news a dying species? One thing is certain. The phone is to news delivery in 2026 what the television set was in 2005. The printed word is still high—or relatively high—on the credibility charts. The challenge for newspapers is to leverage their strong brand equity to engage readers/viewers across multiple digital platforms. Those who do not are writing their own obituaries. Those who do will dominate the media universe in the next decade.

Influencers

These are individuals (supported by strong research and production teams) who have built a large following on social and digital media largely based on their personal brand equity. Influencers share content that aligns with their personal brand image, and hence, the scope still tends to be a little restricted. Often, these influencers have strong personal opinions (biases?) and create content to pander to their core viewer base.

Seemingly Unbranded Platforms

This is the largest base on which social and digital media runs: comparatively unbranded content platforms. Most often, we do not even know the people behind these platforms. Due to paucity of funding, these platforms earn their revenue through digital advertisements. Every click and every view counts. It is unsurprising, then, that these platforms curate what they believe to be the most engaging content online. As the focus is more clicks and views, these platforms are not driven by which high-profile personality features in their content.

Let me give you an example. A top quality speech made in Parliament even by a not-so-high-profile MP could be given the same content space and airtime as, say, an intervention made by a first-rung Opposition leader like Akhilesh Yadav, Rahul Gandhi or Abhishek Banerjee. Both the legacy media and influencers will have to watch out for this alternative, which is sharp to garner more views and clicks.

The three different kinds of outlets carrying political content do not really need to jostle with each other. It's not either/or. Legacy media cannot do what influencers are doing. Influencers cannot do what unbranded platforms are doing. Political parties and politicians that can harness the power of all three will win the perception battle. The one constant: content is king.

5

PM Modi Podcast: An Alternative View

In early 2025, the Prime Minister's podcast with a friendly interviewer broke the internet. It was a masterclass in how to attempt to set a narrative. Soft questions. No follow-ups. A popcorn Q&A, then coated with caramel and served up by news platforms falling over each other to please the executive chef. The key words from the podcast were then plated, garnished and impeccably presented as headlines, tweets and tickers across the media smorgasbord.

Here are some of these keywords from that sugary podcast, with an alternative view.

1. Himalayas (#EmbracingTheSolitudeOfTheMountains)

- The Prime Minister gave a ten-minute answer on the podcast where he explained how he sought the higher purpose of living—testing his bodily strength in that pursuit. All very noble.

  To wax eloquent about a supposed 'elevated living' is quite insensitive and tone-deaf for a PM under whose leadership people have (what can only be described as) the opposite of elevated living. Ordinary, *biological* Indians are forced to test bodily capabilities on a daily basis in the most dangerous ways and lose their lives—all to earn a living.

Between 2014 and 2023, 736 people died cleaning sewers and septic tanks.[393] Sixty-seven lakh children go without food every day.[394] Thirty farmers commit suicide every day.[395]

- The Prime Minister shared that, as a child, he chose to skip a family wedding to take care of a Swamiji who was on fast. Very thoughtful.

  Farmer leader Jagjit Singh Dallewal was on a hunger strike for over 100 days demanding MSP and other rights for farmers.[396] Yet, the Prime Minister never met him. For over a year, protesting farmers camped on the borders of Delhi, their meal plans mostly inconsistent; 750 lost their lives.[397]

2. RSS (#ShapedMyLife)

- While banning RSS, Sardar Patel had famously said, which you might recall: 'Undesirable and even dangerous activities have been carried out by members of the Sangh. It has been found that in several parts of the country, individual members of Rashtriya Swayamsevak Sangh have indulged in acts of violence involving arson, robbery, dacoity, and murder and have collected illicit arms and ammunition.'
- When Mahatma Gandhi initiated the Dandi March and Quit India Movement, RSS founder K.B. Hedgewar declared that the organization would not take part.
- Savarkar justified rape as a political weapon. He submitted multiple petitions for clemency to the British.

3. Criticism (#SoulOfDemocracy)

- Since PM Modi came to power in 2014, how many press conferences has he addressed?

- Since 2014, the Prime Minister has not answered even a single parliamentary question under his name. No question has been balloted for him since 2019 in Lok Sabha.
- Under his watch, critics and activists have been arrested under laws like UAPA, with conviction rates of only 2.54% between 2014 and 2022.[398]
- Siddique Kappan. Father Stan Swamy. Umar Khalid. What about their incarcerations?

4. Heritage (#DepthOfOurHeritage)

- 'Rationalization' of textbooks erases Muslims from India's history. Mughal history in grades seven to twelve is now severely limited, with minimal coverage of its emperors and historical texts.
- The eleventh-grade history textbook included the sentence, 'Mahatma Gandhi was convinced that any attempt to make India into a country only for Hindus would destroy India', but it was subsequently removed. The explanation offered: 'The contents of textbooks have been modified to help students build a positive mindset to develop an innate understanding of the drivers of social changes …'
- In 2022, when activists protested communal remarks made by BJP leaders, the Uttar Pradesh government responded by demolishing homes. The chief minister's media adviser shared an image of a home being demolished and tweeted: 'Unruly elements remember, every Friday is followed by a Saturday.'

5. Education (#ChildrenNotTrophies)

- Half of eighth grade students in rural areas across the country struggle with basic division,[399] a skill typically taught in third and/or fourth grade.

- The Union government's expenditure on education in 2025 Budget is 0.37% of the GDP.[400] This is way below the target of 6% set in the much-touted New Education Policy (NEP).

6. Youth (#OurGreatestAsset)

- Eighty per cent of those unemployed are the youth.[401]
- Seventy-five lakh youth enter the labour force every year. However, only four out of ten possess formal skills.[402] Half of all graduates are not immediately employable.[403]

7. Gujarat Riots (#Denial)

- Fact 1: In April 2004, the Supreme Court said, 'Modi was like a modern-day Nero who looks the other side when helpless children and innocent women are burned.'[404]
- Fact 2: Over 1,000 were killed, 223 more people reported missing and another 2500 injured during the violence that followed in Gujarat in 2002.[405]
- Fact 3: Bilkis Bano's rapists were released by the Gujarat government.[406]

8. Trump Connect (#NationFirst)

- Enough said.

SPEECHES

1

Excerpts from Rahul Gandhi's Motion of Thanks on President's Address in Lok Sabha

Victory to the Constitution!

We have collectively fought to protect the Constitution. So, it's quite good to hear the BJP MPs chant 'Constitution, Constitution' every two minutes. For the last ten years, there has been a systematic attack on the Constitution, on the idea of India, on anybody who opposed the government, and on millions of people who resisted the ideas being proposed by the BJP. Many of us were attacked personally. Some of our leaders are still in jail. Not only the Opposition, but anybody who resisted the idea of concentration of power, of concentration of wealth, of aggression on the poor, Dalits, minorities and tribals was crushed violently. I, myself, was attacked by order of the Government of India. There were twenty-plus cases and a two-year jail sentence against me. My house was taken away. There had been 24x7 attacks on us in the media. When there is an attack like this on you, you obviously need refuge, a place or ideas to defend you. So, I want to start my speech today by telling my friends in the BJP and RSS about the ideas which the entire Opposition used to defend the idea of India. From where did these ideas come and how did they give all of us who opposed this regime the strength to fearlessly take any onslaught which was placed before us.

I would like to start by showing an image of our refuge—Shiv ji. The first idea in this image, that we defend, is the idea of confronting our fear. Shiv ji places death one inch from his neck and that is the spirit with which we fought. We are still in the Opposition. I am happy and proud to be in the Opposition because for you, there is only power. For us, there is truth, and this is the symbol of truth. So, when Shiv ji places the snake near his neck, what he is saying is: 'I will accept the truth and I will not back down from the truth.'

Behind the left shoulder of Shiv ji there is the Trishul. I would like you to understand that there is a reason that this Trishul, a weapon, has been placed behind his left shoulder. The Trishul is not a symbol of violence, it is a symbol of non-violence and that is why it is placed in a place where Shiv ji cannot reach with his right hand. When we fought the BJP, we were non-violent.

There is a third and very powerful idea that emerges from truth, courage and non-violence. It is a symbol that many of you hate but that idea is the Abhaya Mudra, the symbol of the Congress Party. As Mahatma Gandhi ji used to believe, it is not good enough to not be scared, it is not good enough to use non-violence—it is also important that you make others not scared and make them fearless. These two ideas were used by all of us when we fought the Britishers and they were put forth by Mahatma Gandhi ji. The Prime Minister, of course, has a direct connection with God. The Parmatma speaks to Modi ji's aatma directly, unlike with all humans. We are all biological. The Prime Minister is a non-biological being. The Prime Minister also said that Gandhi is dead and Gandhi was revived by a movie. Can you understand the ignorance when someone says that Gandhi is dead and a *movie* revived the Father of the Nation?

Not one, but all our religions talk about courage. In the Quran, the Prophet (Peace be upon Him) said: 'He [God] said: 'Have no fear! I am with you, hearing and seeing.' Let us come to Sikhism, a community the BJP attacks every day. Guru Nanak ji also shows the Abhaya Mudra and says, 'Do not be afraid and do not instil fear in others.' The image of Jesus Christ also shows the Abhaya Mudra. He said, 'If someone slaps you on one cheek, turn to them the other also.' Buddha also shows the Abhaya Mudra, so does Mahavir.

Therefore, Hindustan has three foundational ideas. All the great leaders of our country have believed in the principle of 'do not be afraid, and do not instil fear in others'. The Hindu religion clearly states that one should stand with the truth, not retreat from the truth, not be afraid of the truth. Ahimsa is our principle.

~

Lord Ram's birthplace sent a message to BJP, and that message is sitting right in front of you [Awadhesh Prasad, Member of Parliament, Faizabad].

I asked Awadhesh ji, 'When did you realize you were winning the polls in Ayodhya?'

He said, 'I knew from the very first day.'

Then I asked, 'How did this happen?'

He replied, 'Rahul ji, they are building an airport in Ayodhya. The land of the people of Ayodhya was taken away, and to this day, they haven't received any compensation. All the small businesses and shops in Ayodhya were demolished, and the people were thrown out onto the streets. Everyone else was invited for the inauguration except the people of Ayodhya.'

This was the reason for his victory. In the hearts of the people of Ayodhya, Narendra Modi ji took away their land, demolished their homes, and then didn't even allow the poor people, farmers and labourers of Ayodhya to attend the temple inauguration. Forget attending the inauguration, they weren't even allowed near it. So, the people of Ayodhya sent the right message.

~

The BJP spreads fear. In response, the Opposition organized the Bharat Jodo Yatra, bringing the entire country together. During the yatra, we heard a lot about the fear you have spread. While we were walking, a woman approached me and grabbed my hand, looking nervous.

She told me, 'My husband is beating me.'

I asked, 'Why?'

She replied, 'Because I couldn't provide breakfast in the morning. Because I couldn't afford it, due to inflation.'

I asked, 'Sister, how can I help you?'

She said, 'Please don't do anything. Just remember this—that because of inflation, thousands of women across India are being beaten every morning.'

You have instilled fear in the minds of millions of women across India due to inflation.

~

A few days ago, I met with the family of an Agniveer in Punjab, who was martyred in a landmine blast. I call him a martyr, but the Indian government does not. Narendra Modi ji calls him an Agniveer. He is given just six months of training, while on the other hand, Chinese soldiers receive five years of training. You hand him a rifle and place him on the front lines, instilling fear in his heart. You create a division between soldiers—one will get a pension and be recognised as a martyr, but the other will not. Then, you call yourselves patriots.

~

For the first time in India's history, states have been snatched from the people. You have taken away the statehood from Jammu & Kashmir and Ladakh. You have drowned Manipur in a civil war. You and your policies, your politics, have set Manipur on fire. Till today, the Prime Minister of India has not visited Manipur. It seems as if Manipur is not a part of India.

The Prime Minister says that he has a direct connection with God. Maybe God sent a message saying, 'Modi, implement demonetization.' Small and medium businesses, which are the backbone of India's employment, were wiped out. First, they announced demonetization, then implemented a faulty GST. The income tax department constantly hounds them with GST, demonetization and twenty-four-hour harassment. The government tries to crush their cash flow so that small businesses can perish and billionaires can take their place. I went to Gujarat and spoke with textile owners. I asked them why demonetization and GST were implemented, and they said it was done to help the billionaires. Narendra Modi works for the billionaires. It's a simple fact. So, this time, you will lose in Gujarat. You can write it down. The INDIA alliance will defeat you this time in Gujarat.

~

We introduced the Land Acquisition Bill to protect the land of farmers and ensure they get proper compensation. You tried to abolish it, but couldn't. So, in every BJP-ruled state, you have gotten rid of it. The Prime Minister told them that the Farm Bills are for their benefit. The truth was that these laws were for the benefit of Adani and Ambani. Seven hundred farmers were martyred. We asked for a moment of silence for farmers in this House. You didn't allow that because, according to you, they weren't farmers; they were terrorists. The farmers requested that if 16 lakh crore rupees can be waived off for billionaires, then please give us a little consideration too. The farmers requested that if every product gets the right price, then we should also be given MSP. This was their only request. But you refused waivers and MSP for farmers.

Let's come to students. You privatized the public sector and blocked the path. National Eligibility cum Entrance Test (NEET) is not a professional exam; NEET is a commercial exam. A student can be a topper in NEET, can excel, but if they don't have money, they cannot get into a medical college. The passing percentage in NEET is 20–22%. This entire exam has been designed for wealthy children. In the last seven years, there have been seventy paper leaks in these commercial exams. The Opposition requested for a one-day discussion on the NEET Scam. However, the government says no, there will be no discussion on this.

The BJP has instilled fear in the army, among the youth, farmers, labourers, women and the disabled. There is fear within their own party as well. That is the reason why you are not defending yourself. You are completely silent. You cannot defend yourself.

~

When I became the LoP [Leader of the Opposition], I realized something which is also on the lines of the principles of Shiv ji. The idea was that after becoming LoP, all my personal dreams, my personal aspirations and my personal fears have to be put aside. I am actually two people. I am a Constitutional person and my job is to be the Leader of the Opposition, to represent all these parties equally. So, when Hemant Soren ji is in jail or Kejriwal ji is in jail, it should disturb me; it should hurt me. When you unleash your agencies on elected leaders, it is my job to defend them. The people have given me a responsibility that should overcome my personal likes, dislikes and aspirations.

Speaker sir, why I am saying this, is because when you were being put in that Chair, I walked with you to the Chair. I shook hands with the Prime Minister and I shook hands with you. Speaker sir, there are actually two people sitting in that Chair. There is the Speaker of the Lok Sabha and there is Mr Om Birla. When I shook your hand, you stood straight and shook my hand. But when Modi ji shook your hand, you bowed down and shook his hand. You are the final arbiter of the Lok

Sabha. You are the final word here. What you do and say fundamentally defines Indian democracy …

Finally, I would like to say that the principles that allowed us to fight are in our traditions—truth, courage and non-violence; and they are all in our religions. My recommendation to the NDA, if you take it, is that this country has a government and you are the government. And you are—whether we like it or not—the Government of India. But I would say to you that as individual members and as the [Union] cabinet, you should not spread fear or hatred in this country. When the Opposition says that let us have a debate for one day, have it, as it is not going to harm anybody. Do not take us as your enemies. We are sincerely here to make your work easier as long as you follow the basic principles. I would say that we both want to work for this country, work with the spirit of bravery, work without violence and work without hatred.

2

Excerpts from Abhishek Banerjee's Speech on Union Budget in Lok Sabha

If I were to describe this Budget in one line, I would call it a Budget without any clarity or vision, which has been rolled out to satisfy the coalition partners of the BJP, rather than providing any substantial relief to the 140 crore people of this country. This Budget was planned by two individuals to keep another two in good faith, neglecting the aspirations of 140 crore people.

What we now have in place is a creaky, shaky coalition. Coalition means cooperation, collaboration and cohesion … No one is referring to this government as Modi 3.0 … The message from the electorate of this country is loud and clear. Times have changed. Today is exactly the fiftieth day since this rejection. But Prime Minister Modi refuses to accept this reality. He wants everyone to believe that 'all is well'. So, the Defence Minister is the same person; the Commerce Minister is the same person; the Home Minister is the same person; the External Affairs Minister is the same person; the Finance Minister is also the same person. But, one thing has changed. The cheerleaders have gone down in number.

Amidst all the failures in the last decade, the PM and his government have achieved something which is truly remarkable—a world-class collection of abbreviations. There is ART, which means Accountability, Responsibility, Transparency. There is HRIDAY, which means Heritage City Development and Augmentation Yojana. There is GOBAR, which means Galvanizing Organic Bio-Agro Resources. They have thrown every absurd acronym possible at the people of this country. There are 110 names! I want to reply to this government in a language which this government understands.

So, B.U.D.G.E.T. I will explain all six letters in detail.

Let me start with 'B'—'B' for betrayal.

BJP promised 'acche din'. But what have they done? They have betrayed the citizens, the housewives, the daily wage earners and the farmers. A home-cooked vegetarian thali costs 8% more year on year in April 2024. The price of onions goes up by 43%. The price of tomatoes goes up by 41%. The price of potatoes goes up by 39%. The price of an LPG cylinder prices crossed 1,100 rupees in 2023. Household savings plummeted to a fifty-year low in 2023, with household debt reaching a record high of 39.1% of GDP in 2024 ... If the NDA government in the last ten years had spent even a quarter of time—which it dedicated to political witch-hunting and spreading communal hatred—on addressing the real issues of interest for the people, India would not be ranked 111th out of 125 countries in the Global Hunger Index. Crimes against Scheduled Castes (SC) and Scheduled Tribes (ST) have increased by 13% and 14% respectively from 2021 to 2023. They speak about a double-engine government in Uttar Pradesh. But let me give you a data point which was given by the Ministry of Social Justice and Empowerment last year. It proves that Uttar Pradesh has the highest number of cases of atrocities against Dalits, followed by Rajasthan. Who is in power in Uttar Pradesh and Rajasthan?

Talking about vacancies in tribal schools, about 10,000 vacancies in Eklavya Model Residential Schools remain unfilled, as of today. Coming to religious representation, the whole country needs to know that BJP does not have a single Muslim MP in Lok Sabha, Rajya Sabha or any State Assembly.

'U' stands for unemployment.

The unemployment rate in our country rose to an eight-month high of 9.2% in June 2024. Among graduates, unemployment was 13% in 2022-23. The Skill India Mission aimed to train 400 million people by 2022, but only 14 million received training by 2024. The target still remains a distant dream.

Unemployment rate for women living in urban India is 22.7%. They speak of 'Beti Bachao, Beti Padhao', but they forget to mention about 'Beti ko naukri dilao'. But look at West Bengal. Kanyashree Scholarship Scheme touched the lives of 85 lakh girls, and won the UN Public Service Award. Over 2.2 crore women have been financially empowered through schemes like Lakshmir Bhandar. Financial assistance of 12,000 rupees annually for general category, and 14,400 rupees for women of SC/ST categories have been provided. Only three states in the country have enterprises where women own more than three out of ten establishments, and these three states are Telangana, West Bengal and Karnataka. It is not coincidental that all three states are governed by the non-BJP political parties. BJP and women empowerment simply do not align, and are rather paradoxical.

I now come to 'D', which stands for 'deprive'.

You spend 20,000 crore rupees on revamping Central Vista. You did this to improve the homes of the rich, influential and powerful.

Over the past decade, the BJP-led Union government has made its Bangla-virodhi stand abundantly clear by deliberately depriving people and abusing power to suppress Bengal's voice. They have made an array of hollow promises, disrespected Bengal's culture and hatched continuous conspiracies to tarnish the state's image. The honourable Finance Minister gave a statement today in the Rajya Sabha, saying that Bengal has failed to implement the scheme that Centre has aided in the last ten years. I challenge the honourable Finance Minister if she can release the White Paper detailing how many rupees the central government has given to Bengal after its embarrassing defeat in the West Bengal Legislative Assembly elections in 2021. Official interactions with the honourable Prime Minister and the other BJP ministers were met with a dismissive attitude and constant rejection. Our leaders fighting for the people of West Bengal were detained in Delhi. Women MPs were manhandled and dragged by their hair. And BJP talks about naari shakti!

The Finance Minister yesterday in her speech proposed flood control initiatives for states like Bihar, Assam, Himachal Pradesh, Sikkim and Uttarakhand. Unsurprisingly, West Bengal was once again left out in spite of the northern part of West Bengal being one of the worst flood-affected areas and despite the fact that six out of eight MPs from parliamentary constituencies that fall under the northern part of West Bengal are from BJP. I hope people of Jalpaiguri and Alipurduar are watching this, and listening to what I am saying.

This government is depriving the students. The inability to conduct NEET is one of the biggest failures of this government, jeopardizing the future of almost 33 lakh bright students. More than 12,000 vacancies in Kendriya Vidyalayas nationwide are yet to be filled. There are more than 7,50,000 vacancies for teaching posts nationwide from Class I to Class VIII. There are more than 1, 20,000 vacancies for teaching posts in Uttar Pradesh alone from Class I to Class VIII. Students account for 8% of the total number of suicide victims. Lives of more than 13,000 students are lost every year because of suicides.

Now, I come to 'G' for 'Guarantee'.

The Prime Minister announced demonetization and guaranteed that black money would be wiped out. Ninety-nine per cent of the black money came back into circulation and is in the system now. He guaranteed that terrorism would be curbed. There have been twenty-six terror attacks in Jammu & Kashmir in the last six months. He guaranteed to create 25 crore jobs in 2014 and he failed to do it. In 2023, the government admitted that only 1 crore jobs were created in the last ten years. They guaranteed to turn bullet trains into a reality by 2022, but failed again. The deadline has been conveniently shifted and postponed to 2026. They had guaranteed to double farmers' income by 2022. The actual growth staggers at 3% and, at this rate, the farmers can expect their incomes to be doubled by 2035 or 2040. Around thirty farmer suicides happen every single day.

'E' stands for eccentric.

The Prime Minister's obsession with grandstanding has only distracted the countrymen from the real issues, leaving India to pay the price for his eccentricities. The government's abrupt announcement of the national lockdown in March 2020 left citizens with only four hours to prepare and the tragic deaths of over 8,700 people. In 2020, the same Modi government unilaterally passed three contentious Farm Bills without any consultation with the farmers or farmers' organizations or any Opposition parties. Seven hundred farmers died! You people have blood on your hands! In November 2016, the Union government demonetized 500- and 1,000-rupee currency notes. One hundred and thirty fellow Indians lost their lives due to heat and the strain of standing in long queues, falling victim to this eccentric decision.

I come to the last letter, 'T' for tragedy.

When the Kolkata flyover collapsed a few years ago, Modi ji jested that it was not an act of God but an act of fraud. We wonder what he had to say when 141 lives were lost in the Morbi bridge collapse in Gujarat. What happened when roofs of Delhi, Jabalpur and Gujarat airports collapsed? What happened when the Ayodhya Ram temple roof started leaking after the first rain? When Mumbai's Atal Setu started developing cracks within six months of its inauguration? When forty-one workers were trapped for seventeen days after Uttarkashi Tunnel was caved in? When twenty people were killed as a girder launcher collapsed on Samruddhi Expressway in Thane? When 300 lives were lost in the Balasore train accident last year? When nine people were killed and forty people were injured as a goods train rammed with Kanchanjunga Express last month, was it an act of God or an act of fraud? The Railway Minister has blood on his hands. A once reliable mode of transport has been transformed into a death trap. There have been 244 train accidents between 2017 and 2022. There have been fifteen major accidents in 2023 alone.

Manipur suffered for over two years before some form of peace was finally negotiated. There have been more than 200 killings, 70,000 displacements and the wrecking of more than 1,000 homes. Yet, there is no mention of the word Manipur in the Union budget.

Another tragedy of this government has been the weaponization of the central agencies to carry out politically motivated witch-hunts against the Opposition leaders like many of us, including me. They did not stop at me or my wife or my elderly parents or my PA or my advocate, but even my eleven-year-old daughter and four-year-old son were not spared. But the people of West Bengal and the people of my constituency elected me third time with a margin of 7,10,000 votes. If I have to bow, I will bow before the power of the people, but not before the people in power.

I have exposed the track record of this government on promises, governance, guarantees and targets. The election results are a direct audit of the performance of the honourable Prime Minister and this government. The Prime Minister was the face, the body and the head of the BJP campaign which cried, *'Abki baar,* 400 *paar'.* And what is the result of that audit? The result of the audit is that the BJP lost heavily in West Bengal. They were stunned in Uttar Pradesh and were shaken up in Maharashtra.

This takes me back to where I started. Times have changed. The Prime Minister now leads a creaky, vulnerable and shaky coalition, waiting to blow up. Rather than investing in the future of this country, it is unfortunate that the Union government is investing for Modi ji's political survival at the expense of the nation's well-being. The truth is that the honourable Prime Minister is on borrowed time. You all are on borrowed time. Mark my words.

I would like to end by saying—have a little patience and fasten your seatbelt, the weather is about to get rough.

3

P. Chidambaram's Speech on Union Budget in Lok Sabha

I want to thank the honourable Finance Minister for the Employment-Linked Incentive Scheme (ELI) and other ideas incorporated in the early part of her speech. I am particularly happy that she had an opportunity to read the Congress Manifesto and she picked the good ideas on page 11, page 30 and page 31. Copying is encouraged and copying is rewarded in this House. So, please copy a little more.

I have four major things to say. The first is jobs. The Centre for Monitoring Indian Economy has estimated the all-India unemployment rate, in June 2024, as 9.2%. Earlier, the government had a Production-Linked Incentive (PLI). There must be some reason behind introducing an ELI. And, I suspect, the reason was that the PLI scheme did not create the kind of jobs that you wanted to create. So, will the honourable Finance Minister tell this House what is the outcome of the PLI? ELI is an interesting idea, but it does not inspire confidence that you will be able to place 290 lakh people under the ELI that you have described. It should not turn out to be another election *jumla* like your 2 crore jobs a year.

Look at the magnitude of the unemployment problem. The Uttar Pradesh Police Department conducted an examination for 60,244 vacancies. About 48 lakh persons applied and wrote the examination which was cancelled a couple of days later. Air India wanted to fill 2,216 vacancies for handymen. About 25,000 people thronged Mumbai airport for a walk-in interview, and the police had been called to restore law and order. Madhya Pradesh advertised fifteen low-skilled government jobs; 11,000 applications were received. Among them were post-graduates, engineers, MBAs. One of them was a person who had just written an examination to be a judge in the Madhya Pradesh High Court. The best illustration is by the Staff Selection Commission. There are Staff Selection Commissions of the Centre and the States. Uttar Pradesh conducted an examination for 7,500 posts. About 24,74,030 people applied for those jobs. Yet, the RBI, about two to three weeks ago said, 'There is no job crisis in India'. Why didn't anyone from the Prime Minister to any officer reject this statement? The RBI is supposed to be cautious, conservative and neutral. You are cautious, you are conservative but you are not neutral at all. I suggest that unemployment be taken seriously. We will wait for the outcome of your ELI scheme. It is an interesting scheme. At the moment, I am not impressed, I am not convinced; the outcome alone will judge whether your intentions are good, whether you really want to tackle unemployment.

The second subject is inflation. The honourable Finance Minister, in Paragraph 3 of her speech, dismissed the subject in ten words. The Wholesale Price Index (WPI) inflation is 3.4%; the Consumer Price Index (CPI) inflation is 5.1% and food inflation is 9.4%. Mostly, along towns and villages abutting the national highway; at best, the State Highways and at best, the District Highway. But go into the hinterland of India, go into the Kalahandi Balangir Koraput districts of Odisha, go into the interiors of Dharmapuri or Ramanathapuram, the inflation is much higher than your 3.4% or 5.1% or 9.4%. The Chief Economic Advisor who may be cautious, conservative—he has a degree of autonomy which no other officer of the Government of India has—said in his Economic Survey, 'India's inflation continues to be low, stable and moving towards the 4% target.' It has been moving for the last four years. When will it arrive at the 4% target? Is inflation low? Is it stable? If it is moving towards the 4% target, why has the RBI not revised downward the bank rate fixed in June 2023? This is the thirteenth month of a 6.5% bank rate. Bank rate is a good measure of where inflation is moving. If inflation is moving towards the 4% target—4% target is actually four plus or minus two; it is not 4%— assuming that 4% is the target, why is the RBI keeping the bank rate at 6.5% for the last thirteen months? Why is the Monetary Policy Committee not willing to revise it downwards? And, I think, what the Chief Economic Advisor said in his Economic Survey is injury, and the honourable Finance Minister, dismissing the subject in ten words, is adding insult to injury. Inflation is a humiliating situation because every family is hit by inflation. I warn this government. You are not taking inflation so seriously. The last set of by-elections punished you, where out of thirteen seats, ten seats were won by the INDIA bloc. If you don't take inflation seriously, you will be punished more. And, in this situation, you claim that the growth last year was 8.2%, and this year, it will be 6.5% or 7%. I am not going into macro-economic analysis. Some of my colleagues will do that. I ask you, how do you arrive at this growth rate? You take the nominal growth rate and apply a deflator and arrive at the GDP. Sir, the House and you must know that the deflator that they have adopted for the manufacturing sector for last year is 1.7. When WPI inflation is 3.4, when CPI inflation is 5.1, food inflation is 9.4, how do you adopt a deflator of 1.7? In fact, I want the honourable Finance Minister to tell us: What is the deflator you have adopted for manufacturing industry, what is the deflator you have adopted for agriculture and what is the deflator you have adopted for services? Nominal growth is measurable. But your GDP, in real terms, is (measured) simply by adopting a deflator. And if you adopt a deflator, which several knowledgeable economists and experts throughout the world have severely criticized for the last three or four years, you will arrive at this rosy picture. If you would have adopted a deflator less than 1.7, you would not have arrived at 8.2; you would have arrived at 9.2. You adopt a deflator of 0.5, you will even cross 10%. So, please tell us, what is the deflator you are adopting? Why are you adopting and tell us what is the nominal growth rate and how do you arrive at these growth rates?

Growth rates cannot be seen, but can be *felt* by the people. Anyone moving around—the people—will know. When there is impressive growth, when there are more goods and services, when prices are affordable, when there is money floating around in the market, when your pockets are jingling with coins or currency notes, you get the feeling that things are going alright in this country. Do you get that feeling? I travel at least five hundred to thousand kilometres every month by road; I don't get that feeling. Does any member from his constituency or state get the feeling, or do people tell him that 'things are very good' or 'please go and tell the Prime Minister in Delhi that things are very good and we are very happy …' Does anyone get that feeling?

The third subject is wages. The honourable Finance Minister said, 'I have given relief'. Who has she given relief to? I don't grudge the relief. In 2022-23, the last figure I was able to access, the number of taxpayers was 7.4 crore. Out of that, 65% had zero tax liability. They file a return, but no tax is paid. Assuming that the 65% remains constant, out of, say, eight or nine crore tax payers today, five and a half to six crore people would have zero tax liability. You have given relief to people who moved to the new tax regime. I have seen various calculations in the new tax regime. Out of 142 crore people, let us assume you have given relief to 2 to 3 crore people. What about the rest? Do you know the conditions of the rest? The household consumption expenditure survey of the Government of India counted that the bottom 50% have 3% of the national wealth, 13% of the national income, and the monthly consumption of a family in the rural areas is 3,094 rupees. Multiply it by twelve, you would arrive at about 37,000 rupees a year. In urban areas it is 4,963 rupees. Multiply it by twelve, it comes to 60,000 rupees a year. So, we have 50% of the population, that is 71 crore, having a monthly consumption expenditure between 36,000 rupees and 50,000 rupees. Are they rich or poor? This is the bottom fifty, below the median. If you go down to the bottom twenty, or go down to the bottom ten, they are even poorer. What is the relief for them? And the Chief Executive Officer of the NITI Aayog says, India has virtually abolished poverty. Poverty cannot be more than 5%. Poverty cannot be more than 5% when you are talking about seventy-one crore people. Thankfully, seventy-one crore is not 5%. Then India's population would be 1,400 crore. But India's population is 142 crore. One half is 71 crore, and they are below the median, and this is the median income. I ask the honourable Finance Minister: what is the relief given to them? In the World Hunger Index of 125 countries, we are at 111 place. You may not accept the World Hunger Index, but the action that the government has taken, namely, giving free foodgrain to 81 crore people, is a tacit admission that on the Hunger Index, we are very, very low.

My last subject is federalism. What do we see around this country? All-India Service officers defy the directions and orders of the Council of Ministers of an elected government in Delhi. Funds are withheld from Kerala and West Bengal on one pretext or the other. Borrowing limits of non-BJP state governments have been slashed. Tamil Nadu has been denied Disaster Relief Assistance. I ask: why does the Union Public Service Commission (UPSC) have to play a role in the appointment of the Director General of Police of a State? Why should a state government not appoint the vice chancellor of state universities? And, how did this Government treat Andhra Pradesh, Bihar and Odisha before April? The same demand was there. The same Andhra Pradesh Reorganization Act was there. The Chief Minister was a different person. The same Act was there, but for ten years, you treated them differently. For ten years, you treated Bihar differently. When a leader wears one cap, you treat him one way, but when he changes that cap and he wears another cap, you treat him another way. I don't grudge at all if you are giving relief to Andhra Pradesh or Bihar, but what about the other states? We are a federal country. This is the death knell of federalism. You are the Union of India. You are the Union government. You are the government of all the states. You cannot pick and choose one state and deny relief to another state.

I thought the honourable Finance Minister loved Tamil. I missed her quotes from Thiruvalluvar. Maybe she will quote a classic poet in Telugu or Bhojpuri in the course of time. I want her to remember that she was born in Madurai, she had her schooling in Villupuram and she had her college in Tiruchirappalli, and it is very painful, as the chief minister of Tamil Nadu pointed out, that not in one place in her sixty-page speech, did she mention the word 'Tamil Nadu' or 'Tamil'. How many times have you mentioned Bihar? How many times have you mentioned Andhra Pradesh? I have no grudge, but please remember that there are other states in India. Other states have people. Other states elect other governments. They vote against you. Please remember that.

Finally, I have five demands. I demand this and I respectfully ask the honourable Finance Minister to give us answers. If you do not answer this today or in the course of this session or subsequently, it is not as if these demands will die down. These demands will echo everywhere in India where the INDIA bloc has the right to speak and write.

Our first demand is minimum wage of 400 rupees per day for every kind of employment. Two, we demand a legally guaranteed MSP. Three, we demand a write-off of the unpaid balance of interest or instalment of educational loans given up to March 2024. Four, we demand abolition—complete abolition—of the Agniveer Scheme, and, five, we demand that NEET be scrapped, and, if some states want to keep NEET, exempt all other states which do not want NEET. These five demands will echo not only in this chamber but these will echo throughout the country until you concede these demands. Thank you, sir.

4

Mallikarjun Kharge's Motion of Thanks on President's Address in Rajya Sabha

The President is the most important part of the Parliament. We respect her a lot. The President's address is prepared by the government. It was expected from the ruling party that they would present this address as a vision statement and tell how the current challenges will be dealt with, but there is no such mention in the address. There is nothing in it for the poor, Dalits, backwards and minorities. Basic issues have been ignored. The BJP said it will change the Constitution, and that's why the INDIA alliance had to launch a campaign to save the Constitution. The poor, farmers, labourers, the oppressed, the exploited, women, youth supported us in this fight and did a great job of saving the democracy. But even now, there are people with a mindset contrary to social justice. This fight will be completed only when such ideology is uprooted.

In the last decade, parliamentary institutions and traditions have been continuously weakened, and the Opposition has been ignored. We have constantly struggled to put forth our views. The BJP had envisioned such a Parliament in which there would be no Opposition. Otherwise, the post of Deputy Speaker would not have been vacant for the first time in the 17th Lok Sabha. There is a legal provision in the Constitution for Lok Sabha Speaker–Deputy Speaker and Rajya Sabha Chairman–Deputy Chairman, but you kept a constitutional post vacant for five years.

In this very Rajya Sabha, the Prime Minister had challenged the Opposition saying 'Ek akela, sab par bhaari'. The election results have shown that the country's Constitution and people are heavier than everyone. The statues of fifteen great personalities including the Father of the Nation, Mahatma Gandhi, Constitution-maker Baba Saheb Ambedkar, and Chhatrapati Shivaji Maharaj were removed from their places and placed in the back corner of the Parliament building. Millions of people used to come there to pay their homage, but you removed them and pushed them back, fearing that protests would be held there. You removed the statues of Mahatma Gandhi, who brought us freedom, and Dr Baba Saheb Ambedkar, who framed the Constitution. We fought for them. When I was a student, I had fought to get the statue of Dr Baba Saheb Ambedkar installed in front of the Parliament. I appeal to you to install the statues of Gandhi ji, Baba Saheb Ambedkar and Shivaji back to their original places. Do not insult them because it will be an insult to 50 crore SCs, STs, Dalits, the deprived, tribal, and to the entire country and the Constitution.

The Prime Minister just said that people want substance, not just slogans. For the last ten years, the Opposition has been asking the government to do some work too, instead of just raising slogans. They gave slogans like 'Achhe din aayenge', 'Aatmanirbhar Bharat', 'Sabka saath sabka vikaas', '400 paar' and now they have drowned. The 2024 election was an ego breaker. Seventeen ministers of the previous government lost. We had demanded removal of the minister who trampled the farmers with a jeep, but the public themselves trampled him and he lost. The Prime Minister used to call us arrogant, but your arrogance has been shattered. Today, you will not be able to raise the slogan of '400 paar'.

~

The Prime Minister speaks so much. I ask the person who has been showing sympathy for the poor and women: where were you when Manipur has been burning for a year; the women and people there are being harassed and their homes destroyed; did you go there even for a day? You visited fourteen countries, gave hundreds of speeches during elections, but why did you not go to Manipur?

I had also said in my last speech that the BJP government only does politics by diverting the attention of the public from important issues. When we talk about farmers, Modi ji talks about releasing buffaloes. When we speak of dividing the country, Modi ji remembers Aurangzeb. When we talk about unemployment and paper leak, Modi ji remembers mangalsutra and mujra. When we talk about inflation, BJP starts talking about inflation abroad instead of the inflation in the country. When the Opposition talks about the public, Modi ji starts telling his Mann ki Baat. I want to tell the Prime Minister to answer current issues, the public is capable of taking a decision on what happened in history.

I have fought many elections, but for the first time, I witnessed a Prime Minister saying such things in elections. They call him a Vishwa Guru, but their truth has been revealed by the headlines of world's major newspapers. France 24 said, 'Ugly speech but not a surprise'. *The Washington Post* said, 'Modi accused of hate speech towards India's Muslims in an election rally'. CNN (Cable News Network) said, 'Modi's Muslim remarks sparks hate speech accusation as India's mammoth election deepens divides'. We are not saying these [things]; the people of the world are saying this to the Vishwa Guru. The statements made by him during the elections were very hateful.

Everyone has heard these quotes. The Election Commission while announcing the elections on 16 March 2024 said, 'There shall be no appeal to caste or communal feelings for securing votes'. The PM spoke about temples, mosques and other religions 421 times. He spoke 224 times about creating divisions, with terms like Muslim, Pakistan, minorities. In seventy-five years, Prime Ministers belonging to different parties have campaigned for elections, but this is unprecedented. In the seventy-seven days of elections, the Congress gave 117 complaints to the Election Commission, out of which fourteen fourteen complaints were against the Prime Minister, on which no action was taken. During elections, the Congress party's accounts were frozen. We received Income Tax notice just before elections. You talk of level playing ground and when elections come, you close the accounts of the Opposition party! The truth is you tried to harass people, in every way possible but people did not get scared. While our accounts were frozen, the ruling party earned thousands of crores from the electoral bonds scheme, which was illegal.

This government has bought MLAs and toppled governments. If this isn't an insult to the Constitution, then what is? How many governments did you break where we had a majority? You broke Karnataka, you broke Maharashtra, you broke Goa, you broke the government in Manipur. You put two Chief Ministers of the INDIA alliance in jail. Up until elections, Modi ji abused coalition governments. He used to say that it is a khichdi government, and that India's image has been tarnished in the world due to coalition governments. The people of the country forced him to form a coalition government by reducing him to a minority.

The Prime Minister used to say, 'picture abhi baaki hai'. But the climax of this story can be guessed from the developments of last month. NEET postgraduate paper leak, UGC-NET (University Grants Commission National Eligibility Test) paper leak, NEET undergraduate exam cancelled, CSIR-NET (Council of Scientific and Industrial Research National Eligibility Test) exam cancelled, horrific train accident, three major terrorist attacks in Jammu & Kashmir, water leakage in Ram mandir, roofs of three airports collapsed in three days, five bridges collapsed in Bihar in fifteen days, toll tax increased, rupee depreciated considerably, cases of rigging have all come to light. Several (competitive exams) were cancelled due to which the future of 30 lakh students has been ruined. In the last seven years, question papers have been leaked seventy times in the country. On 5 May 2024, the news about the paper leak came from Godhra and Patna, and the government kept hiding it. The Minister of Education refused to accept the incident of paper leak and gave a clean chit to NTA (National Testing Agency). When the allegations were caught in a police investigation, the government accepted after being embarrassed.

You have broken the morale of the youth by bringing an unplanned scheme like Agniveer. There was a big movement of youth all over the country regarding this, but you did not listen to anyone. My demand is that the Agniveer scheme should be abolished. We built agricultural universities, we brought the Green Revolution, we brought White Revolution. We gave reservations to SCs. We gave reservations to STs. You only talk about breaking. This is my opinion. This opinion will remain, as long as there is casteism, untouchability in this country, it will remain. If everything is handed over to the private sector like this, where will the children of the poor, deprived, Dalit, tribal, backward classes study?

Meanwhile, a big scam has come to light, which the government has tried to suppress. On 19 May, the Prime Minister said that the stock market is going to grow rapidly. The Home Minister said that 'Buy shares before 4 June'.

The exit poll came. On 3 June, the stock market broke all records, but on 4 June the stock market fell completely. Investors suffered a loss of 30 lakh crore rupees. The Prime Minister and the Home Minister are responsible for this.

In the end, I would like to say a few things about the country's lifeline, the Indian Railways. Recently, the Kanchanjunga Express accident took place. Before that there was also the Balasore accident. Our railways carry passengers equal to the population of Australia every day. On one hand, the country is being shown the dream of high-speed trains and bullet trains; on the other hand, the government is not able to ensure the safety of citizens. If we raise questions on any accident, the answer we get is how many accidents happened in your time? It would be better if you first fill the more than 3 lakh vacancies in the Railways.

In the last ten years, the poor man has been out of the government's thinking. The government's thoughts are limited to a few rich people. Inflation has spoiled the budget of the poor. The rising prices of petrol, diesel, LPG cylinders, fertilizers, pesticides, milk products, etc., have spoiled the budget of the common man's house.

Modi ji's 2014 slogan was 'Ghategi Mehengai, Badhegi Kamai', but it has made life difficult for villages, poor, farmers and labourers. By imposing GST on everyday things, they [the government] have made them more expensive.

In this very House, a BJP speaker said some derogatory things about the first Prime Minister Nehru ji. It is in the proceedings. If the BJP people would have read Atal ji, they would not have shown such venomous sentiments. In the speech that Atal ji gave in Rajya Sabha on 19 May 1964 on the demise of Nehru ji, he said, 'Humanity is sad today, for its worshipper has fallen asleep. Peace is restless today, its protector is gone. Dalits have lost their support, the apple of the eye of the people has fallen. He was a worshipper of peace, but also a pioneer of revolution.'

If there were leaders like Atal Bihari Vajpayee, this situation would have never arisen. Words like mangalsutra, buffalo, land, etc., would not have come up. These [leaders] are different, they were different—so do not compare each other.

Your job is to break everyone, and our job is to unite.

5

Akhilesh Yadav's Speech on Union Budget in Lok Sabha (Translated)

This is the eleventh consecutive Budget of this government, but hopelessness is reflecting. In fact, the hopelessness is evident even on the faces of those in the Treasury Benches. You should have been celebrating your victory after winning the elections, yet it is clear that you are not. This budget is bereft of anything addressing the issues of the unemployed, the youth and the villages. Those with families understand the struggles of maintaining a household—paying for their children's education, covering medical expenses and managing it all, while grappling with rising inflation. When I see and listen to the people in power, I want to say if everything has improved so much in the last ten years, then where do we stand in the Global Hunger Index?

The government showed a big dream of 'Make in India'. The largest number of MPs are elected to the Lok Sabha from a large state like Uttar Pradesh. But we did not get any major projects. Even the PM comes from UP. I would like to ask whether any IIM (Indian Institute of Management) or IIT (Indian Institute of Technology) has been given to Uttar Pradesh? Not only this, has the Union government given any (other) educational institutions?

I want to know whether any major medical institution has been established. The two AIIMS (All India Institute of Medical Sciences) that were established were on land provided by the Samajwadi Party. Are these AIIMS providing adequate treatment? Dreams were shown that privatization will create jobs. To a certain extent, many things were privatized, but jobs have been decreasing. [The] biggest question is, has the government been able to give rights and respect to the PDA (Pichde [backward classes or OBCs], Dalits, Alpasankhyak [minorities])?

By showing tax collection, you are showing dreams but not answering why exports are declining. How will we recover the trade deficit? In ten years, if we are still standing in the same place and there is no indication of real growth—and now with the results of UP—we can see how much work you have done.

If everything had been alright, would this be the result? You haven't just faced defeat, nor is it just a matter of losing *a few* seats—even the Prime Minister's winning margin has been brought down. The PM wanted to win by a margin of 5 lakh votes or even 10 lakh votes, but what was the 'winning' margin?

~

When I hear the Treasury Benches, I am reminded of these lines:

'Vo jhooth bol raha tha bade saleekhe se, main aitbaar na karta toh kya karta?'

(Translation: He was lying so convincingly, what else could I have done but believed him?)

I remember when the Prime Minister flagged off a bus service from Janakpur, and thirty-five people travelled to Ayodhya. Even then, I had demanded an expressway be built from Janakpur to Ayodhya to ease the struggles of commuters. But the Prime Minister has not acted on this request. The government claims there has been FDI (Foreign Direct Investment) and that mobile phones are being manufactured here, but this is simply not true. The industries in Noida were established under the Samajwadi Party's industrial policy and mobile phones are no longer being manufactured there. There is no 'Make in India' happening. Moreover, Uttar Pradesh has received far less FDI compared to the rest of the country. Accountability of the persons responsible for the projects getting delayed due to cost overruns is sadly absent from the scene. There is a 'double-engine' government, seemingly, still this is the state of affairs. There seems to be a competition in this government between the number of railway accidents and paper leaks—both trying to best each other!

~

We have no issue with you handing out packages for political survival. Go ahead. But if you're building an expressway from Buxar to Bhagalpur, why not connect it to the Purvanchal Expressway in Uttar Pradesh? All it requires is an additional twenty-five-kilometre stretch. You're constructing the Buxar–Bhagalpur expressway to satisfy the people of Bihar, and you should, for the development of the state. But why leave out Pakhanpura, the last village where the expressway ends? Why are you not giving Uttar Pradesh a new expressway? Why are expressways in Uttar Pradesh being funded from UP's budget and not from Delhi's? The Bundelkhand Expressway, built entirely with state funds, was inaugurated by the Prime Minister and already requires repairs. It is a four-lane expressway, constructed by the state government at a cost of over 15,000 crore rupees, yet it operates at a loss due to low toll collection. If there were a connection from Haridwar to Satna, the people of Bundelkhand could also benefit. The most concerning issue, however, is that both the governments in Delhi and Lucknow have compromised on the safety and design of these expressways. According to the Indian Road Congress, the median of a road should be between twelve-to fourteen-metres wide. Take a look at the median on the Purvanchal Expressway—you are putting people's safety at risk every day.

When questions about Ladakh and China were raised, the Samajwadi Party suggested constructing six-lane highways from Lipulekh to Gwalior to facilitate quicker movement of our army to the borders. The government accepted this suggestion. However, the tender was later issued for a four-lane highway. When the construction began, I saw a double-lane paved shoulder being built instead. Just think about it—what started as a plan for six lanes was reduced to two lanes! I don't know who designed that highway, but what about the towns surrounding it? Where will people build drains, raise their houses, or repair the roads? It seems as if the government has intentionally put these towns and their residents in a crisis.

~

The government which used to say that they will double the farmers' income, has completed eleven years of their tenure today. When I listen to many honourable members, they say we are giving MSP. Then why aren't you giving it a legal guarantee? You give it a legal guarantee as well! What are you doing for horticulture crops? Will you give MSP for that? How much will the farmers earn when their incomes double? In the last budget, it was stated that 1 lakh crore rupees would be allocated for agricultural infrastructure across the country, but Uttar Pradesh received nothing from it. Has the government even established one single mandi? This budget claims the government will introduce 109 high-yielding and climate-resilient varieties of crops. I want to ask our minister: how many years have you been working on global warming? What has been accomplished? You attended COP-21 (Conference of the Parties) and made assurances during the G20, yet you've done nothing. Now you talk about 109 high-yielding and climate-resilient varieties. When will you deliver these to farmers, and what arrangements have been made so far? In the second paragraph of your speech, you flipped again. You were talking about resilient farming, then talked about promoting natural farming. The government should tell when will you deliver resilient crops seed, how will the farmers benefit from it and do you have a separate package in the budget for natural farming which many farmers are practising?

You have learnt only this from Parle-G biscuit: inflation and profit. The government has reduced the size of DAP (Diammonium Phosphate) fertilizer sacks over the past ten years. Don't make it smaller than this. When farmers go to purchase DAP, they are forced to buy nano urea. I want to ask the government, what benefit has nano urea actually brought to the farmers?

In the name of investment meets, large-scale events have been organized, which were attended by the President, Prime Minister and prominent industrialists. Apparently, MOUs (Memorandum of Understanding) worth 5 lakh crore rupees have been signed! But what has Uttar Pradesh received in return? Nothing at all. Uttar Pradesh is the state with the highest milk production. To promote production and attract investment, the Samajwadi government decided to support anyone wanting to establish dairy plants, which led to the establishment of [Gujarat's] three Amul plants. But since then, nothing has come from your Government. What have you done for these farmers?

~

Today, Uttar Pradesh is lagging behind, one of the reasons being that it is grappling with the highest electricity prices in the country. I recall an incident where an elderly BJP MLA staged a twenty-four-hour dharna, demanding uninterrupted electricity in the Prime Minister's own constituency. Officials approached me, expressing concern for his health and requesting that the protest be stopped. I took the time to speak with him and listen to his grievances. That very day, I decided that electricity should be available twenty-four hours a day in the PM's constituency. I also urged him, that considering the immense support Uttar Pradesh has provided to the Prime Minister, at the very least, the state's electricity quota should be improved. Eight years have passed since then, Uttar Pradesh gave a Prime Minister to the country, yet the electricity quota remains unchanged …

Even as the farmers continue to struggle and suffer through alarming suicide rates, one of the biggest crises today is regarding jobs. I see new schemes being introduced, but will these schemes provide permanent employment to youth? Do you want to build the futures of the youngsters by offering them a measly 5,000 rupees in the name of salaries? The workforce that you are training by using government funds, I believe even these unsuspecting youngsters will be exploited by corporates. The job of Agniveer is not acceptable to any youth in the country who prepares to enlist in the military. When the scheme was introduced, major industrialists tweeted their support, promising jobs for those who joined. Perhaps the people in power remember this, as even they know the scheme is flawed. That's why the Union government has now asked states to provide a 10% reservation for Agniveers …

I want to quickly end with mentioning just two to three more things regarding UP: I demand the construction of the Chambal Expressway. The longest expressway in the country, the Delhi–Mumbai Expressway, was built at a cost of 1 lakh crore rupees, but UP was not connected to it. Why hasn't Uttar Pradesh been connected to this expressway? There is growing concern about the Ganga River, which remains uncleaned. Just like water in the river flows, the budget allocated for its cleaning has also flowed. Additionally, the best lion safari in the country is located in Etawah, yet the government has yet to initiate its operations, because it was established by the Samajwadi Party, and it took us a long time to get it going off the ground, but we were not given the requisite permissions to start it in time. I hope it will be started soon. It's a great project, the pride of UP, due to which for the first time in Etawah, Asiatic lions are being born, their numbers rising …

In the end I want to say two lines:

'Buniyaad ko nakarkar jo imaarte uthayenge, hum bhi dekhte hain, vo kiss manzil tak jayenge.'

(Translation: We will also see how far they will progress, those who undermine the foundation of India to build their own lofty mansions.)

As for Ayodhya, I don't know who the town planner or the architect is, but when this government changes, if there is one city that will become the most magnificent in the world, it will be Ayodhya.

Thank you.

6

Supriya Sule's Motion of Thanks to the President's Address in Lok Sabha

While the issue of paper leaks was briefly addressed by the Hon'ble President, the proven negligence of the National Testing Agency (NTA) has been overlooked. The sudden and repeated postponement of several key examinations—all in the name of maintaining the sanctity of the examination process—has raised serious questions about competence and accountability of the NDA government. In the last five years, out of the sixty-six exams conducted by NTA, twelve exams suffered paper leaks, affecting 75 lakh youths. Multiple arrests are happening now in the states of Bihar, Gujarat, Madhya Pradesh—interestingly, all NDA-ruled states. The NTA works in absolute opaqueness. It is crucial for us to define the purpose of the NTA and bring in transparency. The 18th Lok Sabha should make transparency its cornerstone. Professionalism of educational institutions such as the National Council of Educational Research and Training (NCERT), the University Grants Commission and universities have been damaged in the last decade. The recent law brought in, as mentioned by the Hon'ble President, is only punitive in nature, neither preventive nor compensatory in terms of the prejudicial impact on the students.

It has been a continual demand of the UPA government for the caste census to be released for perusal by the people of India and their representatives. It is only on the basis of proper study and analysis of accurate data that adequate policies can be made to uplift India. The NDA government has grossly delayed the holding of a Census, gravely affecting policymaking. This is an opportune time for Parliament to pass a law to exceed the 50% cap on reservation. Be it in Maharashtra, or Bihar, or the southern states, the reality of the SCs, STs and OBCs cannot be restricted within the 50% cap. There is no logic for such a limit, which is not even provided for in the Constitution, but applicable due to judicial decisions. Despite the verdict of the country's electorate, the clear signal against the crushing price rise and unemployment, it is crucial for the President's address to include at least the intent, if not the comprehensive action plan of the government to solve the crisis.

According to the India Employment Report 2024, nearly 83% of the jobless population consists of young people. It is also concerning to note that the proportion of educated young people with at least a secondary education among the total unemployed youth has almost doubled from 35.2% in 2000 to 65.7% in 2022. According to a report from *Hindustan Times*, as of April, 712 out of approximately 2,000 students registered for the 2024 placements at IIT Bombay were still seeking job opportunities. This represents about 36% of the student population.

～

This year has marked one of the biggest tragedies caused due to illegal hoardings. The tragic incident in Mumbai where a massive 250-ton hoarding collapsed during a dust storm, leading to the loss of seventeen lives, underscores the broader issue of corruption, inadequate regulation and enforcement around public structures. Year after year, after the first rains, roads in Gujarat collapse. On 30 June 2024, despite the ruling government in power in the state, roads collapsed/sunk in tier-1 cities such as Ahmedabad.

Similar is the crisis that Maharashtra has been facing with waterlogging in low-lying areas and localized flooding of roads. Across these diverse infrastructure failures, a common thread emerges—the need for the government to take a more proactive, comprehensive and accountable approach to infrastructure management.

The Hon'ble President emphasized on green energy and jobs. However, the reality today is starkly different. As per the World Air Quality Report, India is ranked third most polluted country. Almost 70% of the Indian population lives in areas that exceed the country's own national air quality standard. On average, every Indian loses 5.3 years of his life due to pollution, which should be seen in comparison with cardiovascular diseases that reduces the average Indian's life by four to five years, and child and maternal malnutrition reduces by 1.8 years. Between 2013 to 2021, 60% of the world's increase in pollution levels has come from India. If we focus and control the pollution crisis, residents in Delhi would gain twelve years of life expectancy.

I would also like to add that only if the population is at its optimum efficiency, will India grow. As per the survey done in 2018 by the Indian Council for Medical Research, high expenditure on mental disorders is shooting up the families' healthcare budget. The study highlights a profound mental health crisis in India, with mental illnesses accounting for one-sixth of all health-related issues, including conditions such as depression, anxiety, bipolar disorders and schizophrenia. It is pushing 20% of Indian households into poverty. Out of the total household budget on healthcare, almost 20% is on mental care. We need preventive and corrective policy.

~

The Hon'ble President highlighted the Act East Policy of the NDA government showing commitment towards the peace and prosperity of the Northeast region. However, it is global knowledge that Manipur has been experiencing prolonged unrest for the past year; women were raped and paraded. We demanded a discussion even in the 17th Lok Sabha. However, all was done to avoid any discussion, let alone devise any comprehensive plan in the face of escalating violence and destruction of social harmony. Therefore, the 'Act East' policy rings hollow unless there is any intent towards accepting our mistakes and working for regional peace.

The new Criminal Law Bills implemented on 1 July 2024 amidst breach of parliamentary security and demand for discussion on price rise were railroaded in Parliament without any discussion. Increase in the police remand period from fifteen days to sixty or ninety days would prove to weaponize the police by the respective state governments. Retention of solitary confinement despite it being in absolute violation of human rights … The introduction of the power to handcuff without court permission is again moving towards a police state. The 18th Parliament must reconsider the Criminal Law Bills and revise all the provisions in line with the Constitution of India.

Amendments to forest conservation and biological diversity protection forest laws were railroaded without any discussion. The Great Nicobar Project is deeply concerning. The recent bail of both Arvind Kejriwal and Hemant Soren displays the weaponizing of the investigative agencies of the country for political purposes. Huge amounts of government resources are focussed only on suppressing the voice of the Opposition; this is a fraud on the taxpayers money. The 18th Lok Sabha must, in the spirit of consensus and to move ahead, bring in necessary provisions to restrict any government, be it Centre or state, from weaponizing agencies for political purposes.

The Hon'ble President has mentioned about the Farmer Producer Organisations (FPO) networks being made but what cannot be neglected is rather than promises, we need a consultative mechanism where farmers of the country are consulted before taking every decision. The three controversial farm laws have proven that the approach of the government is wrong.

First time in history, the 'Vote from Home' option was made available. Firstly, I would like to congratulate the Election Commission of India for increasing voter penetration. However, there were sizeable cases of malpractices by the NDA leaders and pressure upon the Hon'ble Commission. An important example is that of breaking of parties by defecting and approaching the Election Commission to be called the original party to create a defence to the Tenth Schedule. Weaponizing the Hon'ble ECI to further the interest of NDA is condemnable as it is insulting to the people of India, and inevitably the Constitution of India.

There is a mention that the farmers are unable to take care of expenditure. PM Kisan Samman Nidhi (PM-KISAN) has been launched. I would like to shed some light on the PM-KISAN scheme—which provides a meagre 500 rupees per month to farming families—which is grossly insufficient and fails to meaningfully address the significant economic challenges faced by India's agricultural sector. If there were genuine concerns about the well-being of farmers, it would take far more substantive measures. Foremost, legal status must be granted to MSP. Additionally, comprehensive loan waiver schemes are necessary to free farmers. Furthermore, the government should act to reduce the costs of essential agricultural inputs like fertilizers, seeds and equipment. This could be achieved through higher subsidies and the removal of GST on these critical supplies.

While the government has been working on Ease of Doing Business constantly, it is to be noted that the region-wise discrimination and bias shown by the NDA government is against cooperative federalism.

Even though, as mentioned, that the government is continuously working on extension of farming activities including dairy and fishery, the current payment of 22 to 27 rupees per litre to milk producers is significantly lower than the government announced rate of 34 rupees per litre. Compared to other states, milk producers in Maharashtra receive 10 to 12 rupees less per litre, exacerbating their financial struggles. Adding to the discontent, the government's recent decision to permit the import of 10,000 tonnes of milk powder and remove the import duty has further jeopardized locals. This move is likely to depress rates even more, causing distress among local producers. It has been claimed that there has been construction of 4 crore PM Awas Yojana (PMAY) houses but the CAG audit of the PMAY has revealed several issues, including irregular selection of beneficiaries, diversion of funds, and lack of effective monitoring. These findings suggest that the implementation of the scheme in the state has been plagued by various irregularities, undermining the objective of providing affordable housing to the urban poor. I would like to bring attention towards the construction of more than 3,80,000-kilometre stretch of road under PM Gramin Sadak Yojna (PMGSY). PMGSY-III aims to be completed by March 2025. As we enter the final year of this six-year project, it should ideally be 84% complete if progress were uniform each year. However, the reality is quite different. As of now, only 78,492 kilometres of roads have been constructed, which is a mere 63% of the initial target of 1.25 lakh kilometres. To make matters worse, [only] a 1.15 lakh-kilometre stretch has been approved so far, casting serious doubts on the scheme's timely completion. The situation is particularly dire in states like Mizoram, Manipur and Sikkim, where not a single road has been completed under the scheme. This lack of progress is compounded by a damning report from a standing committee on rural development in 2022, which criticized the quality of the roads as 'completely unacceptable'.

Even if there has been growth in construction of the highways by (a double multiple), the Atal Setu Bridge which was inaugurated just three months ago has already developed cracks. Even more alarming, a half-kilometre stretch of road near Navi Mumbai has sunk by a foot. Despite the state pouring a staggering 18,000 crore rupees into the Mumbai Trans Harbour Link (MTHL), these incidents highlight a glaring lack of proper construction practices. These problems underscore that it's not enough to simply build infrastructure; quality and durability are crucial. Moreover, our national rail network, highways, and overall development lag significantly behind other parts of India, reflecting a need for more comprehensive and robust planning and execution in our infrastructure projects.

As stated by the Hon'ble President that there has been growth of tourism, connectivity, employment, etc., in Northeastern states, I would like to bring to your attention that according to the Ministry of Statistics and Programme Implementation, during the financial year 2018-19, eight Northeastern states had a growth rate lower than the national average. In the financial year 2018-19, the eight Northeastern states contributed only 2.8% to the country's GDP. Most of this share came from Assam. Other states together gave one-third of the contribution. This region is behind other parts of India in many areas like power use, roads and railways, and social and economic development. The Northeast of India has historically been a hotspot for secessionist movements, making it imperative for any governing body to prioritize establishing peace, ideally through political negotiations. The Manipur incident is a reflection of the dearth of any proper intervention by the government to establish peace.

In context of the government's claim that it is working for women's empowerment, the number of women representatives in the Union cabinet reflects otherwise. It is claimed that 3 crore women benefited through Lakhpati Didi Abhiyan, but the significant gender gap in workforce participation cannot be overlooked, especially when there's a young and educated female demographic ready to contribute. It's not enough to rely solely on microfinance schemes. We urgently need more affordable childcare options, safe transportation, flexible work arrangements and measures to address unconscious biases in recruitment and career progression. These are the real barriers that limit women's potential in the labour force. While rural women self-help groups have their role, the challenges faced by working women in urban areas are markedly different and demand targeted solutions.

The free ration and affordable (cheap) rates of cylinder are not as helpful as they are reported to be. Over the past five years, the cost of meals has surged by a staggering 71%, while salaries have only increased by a mere 37%, highlighting an alarming disparity that disproportionately affects households with regular salaried individuals. In Maharashtra, the average cost of a home-cooked vegetarian thali has risen by 71%, with a recent CRISIL report revealing a 7% increase in March compared to the previous year. Particularly troubling are the price hikes of essential ingredients: onions, tomatoes and potatoes, which have seen increases of 40%, 36% and 22% respectively. This stark contrast between rising food costs and stagnant wages underscores the mounting financial pressure on ordinary families.

There have been mentions about how the last-mile delivery approach of the government has supported a lot of families, and specially Adivasis. However, arguably the biggest leader of the Adivasis, Mr Hemant Soren was incarcerated for six months for political reasons.

With the support of the government, 25 crore Indians have come out of poverty. But it's hard to understand how NITI Aayog claims its poverty numbers are accurate when no third party—including the World Bank and the International Monetary Fund (IMF)—supports these figures. NITI Aayog has set its own standards for measuring poverty, but why were these particular standards chosen? They seem to be based on the government's flagship schemes, which then raises questions about their objectivity. The national multidimensional poverty measures look at deprivations across three dimensions—health, education and standard of living, each given equal weight. These dimensions are assessed using twelve indicators that align with sustainable development goals. The indicators include nutrition, child and adolescent mortality, maternal health, years of schooling, school attendance, cooking fuel, sanitation, drinking water, electricity, housing, assets and bank accounts. NITI Aayog's National Multidimensional Poverty Index (MPI) employs the Alkire–Foster methodology to gauge the decline in poverty rates. However, while the National MPI uses twelve indicators, the global MPI only uses ten.

During Covid, the government gave free ration to 80 crore people under Pradhan Mantri Garib Kalyan Anna Yojana (PMGKAY). The 2023 Global Hunger Index paints a stark and troubling picture of hunger in India, ranking it 111 out of 125 countries. This dismal ranking places India behind all its neighbours: Pakistan is at 102, Bangladesh at 81, Nepal at 69, and Sri Lanka at 60. According to the index, 16.6% of India's population is undernourished, and the under-five mortality rate is 3.1%. Even more alarming is the prevalence of anaemia among women aged fifteen to twenty-four years, which stands at an astonishing 58.1%. These statistics are a clear admission of the severe hunger crisis and nutritional deficiencies plaguing the country.

While solar panels are being installed on the rooftops of houses under PM Surya Ghar Muft Bijli Yojana, there are plethora of complaints made regarding the scheme as they are facing problems ranging from installation to the website not working properly. Once we bring in a policy, we must implement it end to end.

I rise today to address some critical concerns that have been persistently overlooked, despite the appreciation for the efforts made thus far. While it is commendable that work is being carried out, there are significant underlying issues that demand more strategic planning and dedicated attention. Merely completing tasks is not sufficient. Maintenance and aftercare are integral parts of any successful project. Unfortunately, this is where we see a glaring deficiency. It is not enough to just perform the work; it must be executed with thoroughness and precision. Only then can it be considered truly complete and effective. What we are witnessing is a troubling trend of enacting laws without proper consultation with the Opposition. This approach not only undermines the democratic process but also results in legislation that lacks broader acceptability and support. The absence of comprehensive dialogue and consideration of diverse viewpoints leads to laws that are perceived as undemocratic and, in many cases, counterproductive. It is essential to understand that the strength of our democracy lies in inclusivity and collaboration. When laws are passed without the involvement and consensus of all stakeholders, they fail to represent the interests of the entire populace. This exclusionary practice is detrimental to the very fabric of our democratic institution. The only aim is just not to complete the tasks but also ensure they are carried out with the highest standards of quality and inclusiveness.

Conclusion

A Fictional BJP Manifesto for the Year 2034

We are in the month of May. The year is 2034. Virat Kohli is the manager of the Indian cricket team. Shah Rukh Khan wins the Filmfare Award for Lifetime Achievement. T-10 has become the most followed cricket league in the world. Elon Musk has sent a manned spacecraft called Musk X to Mars. Diljit Dosanjh wins a Grammy. Sam Altman is advocating suffrage for AI robots. Jhumpa Lahiri bags the Nobel Prize for Literature.

And I am now reading the BJP Election Manifesto 2034. What an impressive cover design. Outstanding layout. With tongue firmly in cheek, here are a few excerpts from the document, along with commentary.

15 Lakh Rupees in Every Account

During the former Prime Minister's first-ever Lok Sabha campaign in 2014, he had promised to deposit 15 lakh rupees into every citizen's bank account. Two decades on, we are pleased to have finally delivered. Just thirty days after we are sworn in, the money will be transferred into your bank accounts. We must also acknowledge the linguistic contribution made by the former Home Minister at the time. He was the first person to use and popularize the term 'jumla' (an unfulfilled promise). We are delighted that this five-letter word has received international recognition, and become the 6,00,001st addition to the Oxford English Dictionary.

BULLET TRAINS

You will recall, the first in the series was launched in 2030, a mere eight years behind schedule. Now that we have connected Mumbai to Ahmedabad, we commit ourselves to launching ten more bullet trains. Seven of these will be in Gujarat: Vadodara, Surat, Jamnagar, Bhavnagar, Rajkot, Bhuj and Vadnagar (the birthplace of former Prime Minister Narendra Damodardas Modi).

DOUBLING FARMERS' INCOME

The dignity and empowerment of farmers have always been one of our top priorities. In 2016, we, 'the party with a difference', made a commitment to double farmers' income by 2022. However, because of certain 'Nehruvian bottlenecks', there was a timeline malfunction (in the language of ChatGPT, this means there was a monumental mess of deadlines). But '*ache din*' are only months away. Sorry, that was autocorrect. Please read as '*achhe din*'.

NATIONAL WAX MUSEUM

We propose the setting up of a National Wax Museum, and shall call it NaMom. One thousand life-sized wax (Hindi for wax is 'mom', pronounced as in 'home') statues will feature in NaMom. These will include, among others, once-prominent television anchors who have since retired to a quiet life in Dehradun.

IMPLEMENTING WOMEN'S RESERVATION

Among all our commitments, this is the easiest to make and roll out. This is our USP, where we use content created for earlier manifestos of our party and dutifully put them in the current manifesto. This makes us the only political party in the world which has a right-wing ideology, but has the generosity and diversity to blend a communist ideology into ours. We call this CPM—Copy Paste Method!

DEMONETIZATION

Where were you on the evening of 8 November 2016? The historic televised speech at 8 p.m. was watched more than any saas-bahu serial in the history of Indian television! We are sure all of you remember the announcement made by the world's most accomplished teleprompter orator. We have commemorated this great occasion with an acronym, GEL. Great Economic Learning. Since then, such a telecast has never been repeated—it won't be for the next 100 years. As any life coach will tell you, the greatest learning is failure.

Postscript: This conclusion is a work of fiction. Any resemblance to any living person or event is merely coincidental. Once in a while, let us remind each other not to take ourselves so seriously.

ACKNOWLEDGEMENTS

This is my fifty-fifth book. The first fifty-two books were quiz and reference books. My two recent books, *Inside Parliament* and *Who Cares About Parliament*, were on politics. Blessed that both were bestsellers.

I must begin by expressing my gratitude to Mamata Banerjee—or Mamata di as we know and cherish her. She has not only been my political leader, but also a teacher, an anchor and a guide, who has taken me through each stage of my political and parliamentary career. I have learnt more from her than any other person in public life.

To Abhishek Banerjee, the National General Secretary of the AITC, whose wisdom belies his age. And to every single member of the AITC family for their dedication and commitment to fighting the good fight. The AITC worker is our most precious asset.

Over the years, there have been many people who have touched my life at a personal or professional level.

All my colleagues at Derek O'Brien & Associates, led by Nayan Chaudhury, who has been rock solid for twenty-five years. Senior associates Ayashman Dey, Chahat Mangtani, Shane Baptiste and Varnika Mishra.

Research associates Ankita Dinkar, Anagha, Dheemunt Jain, and every single member of the team for their sparkle and commitment.

Gratitude to Rila and the original team who set up 'Big Ideas', the audacious quizzing enterprise, in 1992.

To my colleagues in Parliament from different political parties. Many of them do not share my ideology and beliefs but participate in the true spirit of parliamentary democracy.

The Indian Express, NDTV, *Dainik Bhaskar* and *Punjab Kesari*, where some of these essays were first published.

My family is the essential support system within which I live, exist, work and grow. My late father, Neil O'Brien, has remained a big intellectual influence on my life. He didn't live to see these three books on politics and even though he often disagreed with my political views, he was a great believer in the sanctity of Parliament and of legislative debate. He would have read these book carefully.

My late mother, Joyce (Jordan) O'Brien, was the ethical and emotional bedrock of our family. If I could carry even half her clarity and sense of right and wrong into my political life, I would achieve a lot.

My brothers, Andy and Barry, and their families. My friends, most of them for over five decades: Chris, Mike, Pat, David, Wendy, Purvez, Ajay, Sunil, Ashok, Vijay, Sumit.

My daughter, Aanya, is a thoughtful, new-generation young woman. She keeps me abreast with contemporary ideas. She keeps reminding me that young people want to be heard by politicians and not simply be spoken to by them.

Finally, my wife, Tonuca. Now back to Kolkata after a successful medical practice in Boston and New York spanning three decades and, of course, Anjolie and Nondini. I often run thoughts and countless drafts by my wife for her feedback, or, as I call it, 'a medical check'. Her sacrifice has been my greatest strength. I can never thank her enough. Never.

Notes

Scan this QR code to access the notes.

ABOUT THE AUTHOR

Derek O'Brien is a politician, author, television personality and public speaker. His speeches and writings on issues of national importance are discussed widely in the national and international media. He is one of Indian Parliament's most recognizable faces, and a leading and articulate voice of the Opposition.

He has been elected three times as a Member of Parliament to the Rajya Sabha from Bengal, representing the All India Trinamool Congress, and is the party's Parliamentary Leader in the Rajya Sabha.

He has authored over fifty reference books, as well as two bestsellers on politics, *Inside Parliament* and *Who Cares About Parliament*. This is his third book on the subject.